AYLWIN SAMPSON & S

A Cheltenham Companion

Illustrated by Aylwin Sampson

PORTICO PRESS • CHELTENHAM

ISBN 0 905352 06 8

First published 1993 by

Portico Press
33A Tivoli Road
Cheltenham GL50 2TD

Printed by Beshara Press
Ambrose Street
Cheltenham GL50 3LQ

THE HISTORY of every town produces a mosaic of streets, open spaces and buildings which, together with the many activities of the inhabitants, creates its particular image.

Cheltenham's rich heritage, compressed virtually into the last three centuries, presents a complex pattern. The aim of this book therefore is to make it easily accessible.

Information on many aspects of the town's history and features has been so arranged that the reader may absorb as much as is desired, and through the use of heavier type for cross-references be directed to associated entries in the alphabetical sequence.

Help, both literary and technical, in the production of this book has been so varied and generously given that the following can be thanked here by only an inadequate list:

Peter and Gill Barlow
Brian Collins of Beshara Press
Charles Croker of Q E D Technology
Ken Pollock
Derek Tennant of Top Flight
The Summerfield Trust

ALL SAINTS CHURCH

If the 200ft spire had been given to the unfinished tower, as the architect John **Middleton** had intended, it would have put the finishing glory to a church that displays Victorian richness and confidence in the Gothic style to a degree that no other Cheltenham building can match. Dating from 1865-8, its polished granite arcade, its elaborate carving, statuary in canopied niches, and above all the ironwork screen and font cover make this church's interior breathtaking. Add to this the magnificence of the organ cases (**Holst**'s father was organist here), the stained glass by Burne-Jones and a reredos in the chancel carved by Boultons, and All Saints rightfully takes its place as the High Church exemplar of the town.

ALMA HOUSE

The battle of Alma was not one of Britain's greatest victories in the Crimean War, but it has given its name to one of Cheltenham's most magnificent houses. The glorious interior has elaborate classical columns, gold paint picking out detail of cornices and panels, and a grand staircase worthy of a London Club - and that's just the entrance hall! Side by side with this Grecian richness is another style, that of 'art nouveau'. There's a copper hooded fireplace beneath a fanciful romantic idyll of pastoral bliss pipe-playing and daisy-chain making. Some of the doors have coloured glass panels or swashes that could have come from an elegant Edwardian restaurant or luxury ocean liner.

So it is not surprising to learn that this opulence was made by the craftsmen of **H.H.Martyn & Co**, though the designer was the relatively unknown Glaswegian, George Walton. He gave up his job as a bank clerk in 1888 to start a firm of 'Ecclesiastical and House Decorators' on the strength of being asked to refurbish Miss Cranston's Glasgow Tea Rooms.

Alma House dates from 1835, its first owner being an Admiral Watts. However, in 1878 the army - and dentistry - took over in the form of various colonels who also practised there. In 1944 the **Gloucestershire Dairy and Creamery** company bought it; lettings included such various enterprises as accountants, a fish restauranteur and, today, *This England* magazine.

ALMSHOUSES

A town which developed two hundred years ago is unlikely to have examples of medieval philanthropy in the shape of almshouses. Nevertheless Cheltenham can produce one, even if it cannot be proud of the story behind the present location. For in 1578 Richard **Pate** provided for six needy Cheltenham persons aged 60 or over. He built almshouses on land fronting the **High Street** near Rodney Road, including a chapel, orchard and courtyard, ordaining that 'each person shall have a private chamber and a private garden; twice a day to be exercised for one whole hour in hearing divine service; and yearly 40 yards of black frieze shall be distributed to make livery gowns'.

Then in 1811 this settled pattern of life was rudely disturbed. On a questionable pretext the site was sold for £250 to a Mr Smith, who promptly resold it for £2000, and the inmates were found a smaller plot in Albion Street, losing chapel, garden, orchard and courtyard. Their new home can

All Saints
church organ

Alstone Spa

Alma House

still be seen, sandwiched between a pub and **Corals Snooker Hall**, on the busy Inner Ring road.

The residents of the Hay Cottage Homes are more fortunate. Their picturesque accommodation looks out on the flowers and grass of Naunton Park. It was on the 80th birthday of Queen Victoria that the first stone was laid, to provide homes 'for the aged and deserving poor without distinction of sect or religion'. John Alexander Hay and his wife Marianne Louisa made their gift 'as a memorial of their long residence in Cheltenham' according to the carved beam on the facade.

And in St Margaret's Road stands Dowty House, a former orphanage for boys, which in 1958 began a new life thanks to the generosity of many townspeople. Foremost among them was George **Dowty** who instead of having a new Rolls Royce gave £2000 and encouraged the staff of his firm to make small weekly contributions to help the 37 old people who had made this somewhat forbidding Gothic building their home.

ALSTONE

To the west of the town centre, beyond **St James's Square**, lies the area known as Alstone, the site of an early **mill** on the **River Chelt**, and, from 1809 onwards, one of the town's smaller **spa** wells, the Alstone Spa. Although the spa lasted only until 1834, the drinking of its waters was revived in the early years of this century at the house known as Alstone Spa, at the corner of Millbrook Street and Great Western Road, which probably occupies the site of the original spa. The present building dates from 1906, but the wooden annexe to one side of it pre-dates it by three years and was probably erected as a shelter for the water drinkers, to one side of an earlier house. A reminder of the building's former use may be seen in the annexe, for the original pump is still there, clearly visible from the road.

Alstone Spa is overlooked by a **railway** bridge of the disused 'Honeybourne Line' which ran from Cheltenham (Malvern Road) to Stratford. This has now been opened as a cycle and footpath from Lansdown Station to **Pittville**, and forms an attractive elevated walk, from which many Cheltenham landmarks may be seen.

ARCHER, FRED

Fred Archer, one of the most successful jockeys of all time, was born in a cottage off **St George's Place** in 1857, the son of a liveryman and former steeplechase rider. The cottage, which is at the end of a cobbled lane, bears a plaque commemorating his birth there.

Much of Archer's early tuition in riding took place at **Prestbury**, a village to the north of Cheltenham, where his father became landlord of the 'King's Arms' in 1858; but his serious training took place at Newmarket, where, in 1868, he was apprenticed to Mathew Dawson, one of the leading trainers of his day. Newmarket was his home thereafter, as he pursued a meteoric career, becoming champion jockey of England at the age of 17, and maintaining that position for the rest of his short life.

Unfortunately, the strains of his life gradually took their toll on him. He was very tall for a jockey, and had to resort to a sparse diet, constant turkish baths and purges in order to keep his weight low. Endless travelling from one race meeting to another wore him down still further, and his life was dogged by financial problems and personal unhappiness, with the premature deaths of his wife and son in 1884-5.

Eventually, in November 1886, while suffering from typhoid fever, depression got the better of him, and he shot himself at his home in Newmarket, at the age of only 29. So ended one of the most brilliant careers in the history of horse-racing.

ARCHITECTS

Cheltenham is justly renowned for its architectural heritage, a superb mixture of Greek, Gothic, Italian and Norman Revival buildings, with the occasional hint of Egypt and India thrown in for good measure! These buildings were a product of the talents of many different architects, working for private developers in the case of most of the houses, and for various church, school or civic committees in the case of the public buildings. The names of many of the architects are known, although there are still many fine Cheltenham buildings for which no architect's name is known, quite simply because the evidence is just not there!

Although none of Cheltenham's architects were in the class of men like John Nash or Pugin, they do include several who figure in national architectural history. John B. **Papworth** is perhaps the single most important 'name' here, while William **Jay**, with his previous American connections, introduces an unusual note to the town's architectural history. Others were very much local men, often acting as surveyors as well - such men as Rowland Paul, responsible for the 1831 Burial Chapel in what is now the Winston Churchill Memorial Garden (a building with just a hint of Egyptian Revival about it); Edward Jenkins, who designed Suffolk Square; and John **Forbes**, the original architect of **Pittville**. After Forbes's resignation as architect at Pittville, Joseph **Pitt** employed in turn Robert Stokes, who was probably responsible for most of the estate's houses of the 1830s, and Henry Merrett, who is best remembered not for his buildings, but for publishing, in 1834, the best early 19th century map of Cheltenham. Slightly later, two pupils of Pritchett of York made a considerable contribution to Cheltenham, namely Samuel **Daukes** and John **Middleton**, while a number of non-local architects designed churches for Cheltenham in the second half of the century - Frederick Ordish (**St Luke's**), Ewan

Christian (**St Matthew's**) and Charles Hansom (**St Gregory's**).

But perhaps the two names that warrant singling out the most, and for different reasons, are George **Underwood** and Robert William **Jearrad**. Underwood, a little-known figure, who died young, may have been responsible for the whole concept of the **Promenade**, and for its greatest terrace, now occupied by the **Municipal Offices**, while Jearrad, in conjunction with his brother Charles, dominated the world of architecture and development in the town from 1830 onwards. Both men appear to have worked as happily - and successfully - with either the Greek or Gothic style, and their work characterises the variety of Cheltenham's fine architecture.

ARLE COURT

This large Victorian mansion on the west side of Cheltenham is now the headquarters of the **Dowty Group**, having been purchased by George Dowty in 1935 to replace his cramped Grosvenor Place South premises. Since then, many new buildings have been built in its grounds, as the Company has expanded its activities.

The name of the house recalls both the ancient village of Arle, which may have had its own church until the 16th century, and earlier houses elsewhere on the western edge of Cheltenham - the original Elizabethan Arle Court, a part of which survives in the large red-brick Arle Court House in Kingsmead Road, and the early 19th century Arle House, now demolished. Perversely, the site of Dowty Arle Court is not technically part of Arle at all, lying as it does in an area of the town once known as Redgrove, and occupying a piece of land known as the Grovefield Estate. Its site was, however, purchased in 1847 by the same family who owned Arle House, the Butt family; at that time there was probably a farmhouse on the site, which was replaced by the new Grovefield House, which was itself replaced by the present Arle Court, also for the Butt family, in 1857.

Of old Arle itself there are few reminders, apart from a scatter of timbered cottages, such as those in Alstone Lane. The rest of the old village is now taken up with modern residential and light industrial development.

ARMS OF THE BOROUGH

Conspicuous on the facade of the **Municipal Offices** as well as on borough vehicles, the 'dragon and onion' **street lamps** and many other places such as the **Playhouse** theatre, the coat of arms was granted to the town eleven years after its incorporation in 1876. The main symbols on the shield comprise two open books as reminders of the educational institutions in the town, the cross of King Edward the Confessor, the first recorded lord of the manor of Cheltenham, a tree to signify the arcadian character of its avenues and parks, while the presence of two pigeons is a reminder of their role in the discovery of Spa waters. The crest above the helmet has another pigeon perched on a roundel representing those waters, and the motto beneath the shield 'Salubritas et Eruditio' needs very little knowledge of Latin to recognise the twin facets of health and education.

ART GALLERY AND MUSEUM

The Art Gallery and Museum was established in 1899, when **Baron de Ferrieres** donated to the town his collection of 43 Old Master paintings, plus £1000 towards the building of a gallery in which to display them. The new gallery was built on a vacant site to the east of the **Public Library** in **Clarence Street**.

In 1907, two years after the Schools of Art and Science had moved out of their premises on the upper floor of the Library, a museum was established in the rooms that it still occupies today.

The Art Gallery and Museum's collections have grown considerably during the past 90 years, and are among the best in the west of England. They cover all major museum disciplines, but are particularly rich in the Fine and Applied Arts and the archaeology and social history of Cheltenham and the north Cotswolds. Nationally (and even internationally), the most important part of the collection is that relating to the Arts and Crafts Movement of the late 19th and 20th centuries, with furniture, metalwork, jewellery, textiles, books and stained glass by the followers of William Morris, many of whom lived and worked in Gloucestershire. The Museum also has a large area devoted to the history of Cheltenham, including a gallery about one of the town's most famous sons, Dr Edward **Wilson.**

A major extension to the Art Gallery and Museum was opened by HRH The Princess Royal in September 1989. A continuous programme of temporary exhibitions is held, and public facilities include the Cafe Museum, opened in 1991.

ASSEMBLY ROOMS

Although demolished as long ago as 1900, the Assembly Rooms are memorable as an essential part of the spa town's history.

As early as 1734, the dining room of a house on the south side of the **High Street**, just west of Rodney Road, was converted for use as a ballroom for 'the company', as the spa's visitors were known, and this was rebuilt in 1784, possibly to a design by the eminent architect Henry Holland.

1784 actually saw the opening of a second, rival, set of Rooms further east, between Bath Road and Cambray Place, but these were relatively short-lived and had closed by 1807.

Further rebuilding took place in 1809-10, and again in 1815-16, and it was the 1816 building - which was opened in great style by the 1st **Duke of**

Pates Almshouses

the Borough Arms

Hay Cottage Homes

Wellington - that served Cheltenham for the remainder of the century. Here, regular balls and assemblies were held, the visitors could play cards and billiards and, throughout the century, a succession of concerts and events were held, given by such contemporary 'household names' as the musicians Paganini, Strauss and Liszt, and the writers Dickens, Thackeray and Wilde.

In 1816, that part of the building at the corner of High Street and Rodney Road opened as Williams's Circulating Library, which continued in business there until 1896, while the first floor was given over to the exclusive 'Cheltenham and Gloucestershire Club'. There, it is said, the best curries in England were served during Cheltenham's late 19th century heyday as 'the Anglo-Indian's Paradise'.

The social regime at the Assembly Rooms was rigid, and its 'Rules' were strictly enforced by the **Masters of the Ceremonies**. Among prohibitions were the wearing of boots, 'undress trousers' and coloured pantaloons, while 'no clerk, hired or otherwise ...... no person in retail trade, no theatrical or other performers by profession' were to be admitted.

Sadly, despite their glorious past, the fortunes of the Assembly Rooms waned as the 19th century wore on, particularly after the opening of what is now the **Everyman Theatre** in 1891, which robbed the Assembly Rooms of another role that it had assumed in previous decades. The commercial Company that ran the building got into debt, and their answer was to sell it to Lloyds Bank, which demolished the Rooms and replaced them with the present bank, an imposing building in its own right, which visitors sometimes think *is* the old Assembly Rooms!

BANDSTANDS

Cheltenham has not been fortunate in its bandstands. Bearing in mind the extent of the **parks** and the ambience of the town it is surprising that today there is only one worthy of the term. Admittedly the **Pittville Pump Room** has nearby a wooden affair, faintly Chinese looking, but it is of wood with a shingle roof and has neither the size nor the character of a truly Victorian bandstand.

Sadly the example which stood in Imperial Gardens has gone, sold in 1948 to Bognor Regis for £175, but there is still one that measures up to expectations and it is to be found in **Montpellier Gardens**. It dates from about 1895. Here is a profusion of cast iron decoration, similar in its panels to those of a verandah of a house in Thirlestaine Road. The incorporation of women's heads has led some to believe this to be a tribute to Queen Victoria, but in fact the design came from a patternbook produced by the Coalbrookdale Company at Ironbridge. The base of the bandstand served as a store for the Archery Club when it used the gardens in Edwardian times, and during the World War II housed the winch for one of Cheltenham's barrage balloons.

BANKS

There are some fine examples of what are termed 'High Street Banks' in, predictably, the **High Street**. At the junction with Rodney Road, standing on the site of the **Assembly Rooms** is Lloyds', dating from 1900. Its designer was F.W.Waller, whose **Town Hall** has a family similarity; it cost £18000. Nearby at the corner of Cambray Place, the Natwest building is worth study as a good example of 19th century conversion, while at the **Promenade** corner there is another instance of the heavyweight classical style so popular in Edwardian times, though in fact it was built in 1880 for the Worcester City and County Bank, being designed by W.H.**Knight**. Later it became the Midland.

But for reminders of the town's changing history, in the High Street the C & A shop retains much of the facade of the old County of Gloucester Bank, known in the 19th century as 'Pitt's Bank'. It was in 1825 that John Gardner, owner of the **brewery**, and partner with Joseph **Pitt** in this bank, had to make a hasty trip to London for money to avoid a 'run on the bank', and in 1888 the bank accepted £5,400 if the Borough Council would take responsibility for the **Pump Room** and gardens in settlement of Pitt's death debt of £10,800.

In **Clarence Street** too, the front of the Cheltenham and Gloucestershire Bank can be recognised by its pair of niches with later sylph figures in them.

But the finest bank buildings architecturally and historically are to be found in **Montpellier**, where Lloyds' occupy the Rotunda, formerly **Montpellier Spa**, and the branch of the Natwest has the delightful conversion at the northern end of Montpellier Walk once known as Hanover House, its decorative **caryatids** providing a foretaste of those to be seen further along. A third example is Barclays Bank at the southern end, known as Montpellier Exchange. It dates from 1843, replacing the museum of Mawe and Tatlow, an establishment owned by a mineralogist, John Mawe, which exhibited statues, alabaster vases and models of Egyptian obelisks.

BARNETT, JOHN

Son of a Prussian diamond merchant and a cousin of Meyerbeer, John Barnett was born in 1802 at Bedford. After a varied career in London as singer and impresario, he came to Cheltenham in 1841. Here he set up as a singing teacher, becoming very successful. The large house, 'Cotteswold', which he bought still stands on **Leckhampton** Hill. Sometimes called the 'Father of English Opera', it is chiefly through his 'Mountain Sylph' that he has a claim to that description. Even if the original work is hardly ever performed today, the parody based on it is, for 'Iolanthe' by Gilbert and Sullivan owes much to John Barnett. His son, Domenico, taught piano at the **Ladies College** and his two daughters became notable singers. He died in 1890 at 'Cotteswold'.

BAYSHILL ESTATE

Some of Cheltenham's finest early Victorian terraces and villas may be seen in the streets of the Bayshill Estate, particularly in Bayshill Road, Parabola Road and St George's Road.

The whole area was originally the property of the **Skillicorne** family, and at its heart was the **Royal Well, Well Walk** and Royal Well Gardens. However, despite the rapid building development of **Montpellier, Lansdown** and the **Promenade** from around 1800 onwards, the estate's owner, the Reverend Richard Skillicorne, adamantly refused to sanction its sale as building land. Not until after his death in 1834 could his widow and son launch plans for a new estate. In the spring of 1837, they began their work by creating what is now St George's Road, and by selling at least some land to builders. Soon, however, they completely changed their approach, and in December 1837 they sold the entire property for £50,000 to a joint-stock company, called the Bayshill Estate Company, which had been expressly formed by a group of local gentlemen in order to develop the estate.

Although the Estate Company was dogged by ill-fortune in the ensuing years, including the slow take-up of much of the land and the financial difficulties of several of its Directors, the new estate gradually took shape, and the best of its houses date from 1837 to 1850. Among these are the three great terraces in St George's Road: Royal Well Terrace (1837-40) nearest the Promenade, has excellent Corinthian details, while Bayshill Terrace of 1838-40 (now largely occupied by the George Hotel) is distinguished by its one surviving first floor portico; the sites of the other two, which had to be removed earlier this century, may still be made out. Of historic interest is the fact that **Cheltenham College**'s earliest premises, occupied 1841-43, were at Nos 7-8 Bayshill Terrace. Beyond Bayshill Terrace, and in remarkable architectural contrast to it, is the Italianate York Terrace of 1846-50.

Bayshill Road exhibits a similar architectural variety. On its west side is a succession of large and imposing villas of 1837 onwards, now converted for use as offices, while on the east, in addition to the rather weak entrance to **Cheltenham Ladies' College** (replacing a number of 1840s houses), is the stone-fronted Royal Parade of 1845-50, which despite its late date is as close to a Bath terrace as any in Cheltenham; it has particularly attractive ironwork. At the top of Bayshill Road, in Parabola Road, is Queen's Parade. Begun in 1839, its building came to an abrupt halt in 1846 with the bankruptcy of its builder, William Swain. For almost 140 years the terrace remained unfinished, and only in the mid 1980s was the existing projecting Corinthian-style house at its east end matched by a similar house at its west end, thereby completing the terrace. The fact that the terrace had not been completed earlier is a good indication of how much the land market was over-supplied during the euphoric days of the mid 19th century.

One final feature of the estate must be noted. The west side of Montpellier Street (formerly Old Well Lane) lay in Bayshill, and Rotunda Terrace, now a row of shops and pubs, was built in 1844-50 as part of a concerted effort to create a purpose-built shopping area at Montpellier. Like Queen's Parade, this terrace has also been successfully extended in recent years, as part of the **Montpellier Courtyard** development.

BAYSHILL UNITARIAN CHAPEL
Placed prominently near **Royal Crescent** and **Cheltenham Ladies' College** in the appropriately named Chapel Walk, it was built in 1842-4 and is notable as the first building in Cheltenham to be constructed in the Anglo-Norman style. The chapel was designed by a London architect, H.R. Abraham.

The Unitarian congregation, which was first established in Cheltenham in 1832, now meets in the former schoolroom at the rear of the chapel, the main part of which is now used as an auction sale room.

BEALE, DOROTHEA
Though not the Founding Principal of **Cheltenham Ladies' College**, it is Dorothea Beale whose name is most immediately and powerfully associated with its development and success. Her father was of Gloucestershire stock, and the family property was at Chalford in the south of the county. Her mother was of Huguenot ancestry. Educated at home, then for a year in Paris, she became at 17 one of the first students at 'Queen's College', that institution for women attached to London University.

Such experience and subsequent headship of the Clergy Daughters' School at Casterton - pilloried by Charlotte Bronte as 'Lowood' - led to her appointment in 1858 to Cheltenham. Under her guidance and inspiration the College of today took shape, moving into its new Montpellier Street buildings in 1873.

Not only were bricks and mortar her concern but she also built up associations beyond Cheltenham; with John Ruskin who gave to the library, and St Hilda's Oxford but two examples.

When she died in 1906 her estate was bequeathed to the school, and an example was left that is forever 'Cheltenham Ladies' College'. Even those inaccurate lines tell something of her dominating personality:

Miss Buss and Miss Beale
Cupid's darts do not feel:
How different from us
Miss Beale and Miss Buss.

BEAUFORT HOUSE

One of the finest houses on Montpellier Terrace, it was built in 1826 and served for some years as a boarding house for **Cheltenham College**; indeed so well liked was it that when the boys left two masters stayed on. However there was a less attractive episode when it became the Cheltenham headquarters of the British Union of Fascists during the 1930s, Sir Oswald Mosley addressing a rally and march from its porch.

BERKELEY FAMILY

If one family may be said to have dominated the social and political life of Cheltenham during the early 19th century, it was the Berkeleys, whose leading member was Colonel William Fitzhardinge Berkeley (1786-1857) of Berkeley Castle. 'The Colonel', who later became Baron Segrave (1831) and Earl Fitzhardinge (1841), spent much of his time in Cheltenham, and gathered around himself a body of like-minded men and women, who shared his enjoyment of the good life. He was a great supporter of the Cheltenham Races, and was also master of the Berkeley Hunt, one of the county's most important, which had its kennels in North Place. The theatre was his other great passion, and both he and his brothers often appeared on the stage of the Theatre Royal. Inevitably, he came into conflict with Cheltenham's growing Evangelical lobby, and particularly with the Revd Francis **Close**, who opposed virtually everything the Colonel supported, while his apparent moral laxity - he maintained a number of mistresses, including more than one in Cheltenham - led to further criticism. Eventually, however, his own attitudes began to change, and in the last 20 years of his life he made a very positive contribution to the life of Gloucestershire, serving for a time as Lord Lieutenant.

Politically, the Colonel was a staunch Liberal, and his influence was such that his brothers and cousins were installed as Members of Parliament for a number of Gloucestershire seats. In Cheltenham his cousin, Craven Berkeley, served as M.P. in 1832-47, 1848 and 1852-5, and the rivalry between Liberal and Conservative in the town was sufficient to make the place a political 'hotbed' for many years.

BETHESDA METHODIST CHAPEL

This small stone-fronted Gothic Revival chapel in Great Norwood Street was built in 1845-6 to replace a smaller chapel on the same site. It served

National Westminster bank, High Street

C & A shop
former County of
Gloucester bank
High Street

Miss Dorothea Beale

the busy artisan streets around Bath Road that went under the name of **South Town**.

BILLBROOK HOUSE

Clarence Road is rightly celebrated as the birthplace of one of Cheltenham's famous sons, Gustav **Holst**, but the terrace concerned has other interest too. Billbrook House and its neighbour 1 Pittville Terrace were built in mock Gothic in 1832 for George Dinsdale, becoming a 'private academy' run by Anna and Harriet Heaven. Clearly, Joseph **Pitt** the landowner feared less than angelic behaviour from the pupils for he insisted on compensation for any damage done to his **Pittville** Park!

However he need not have worried, for the school did not last long, and the houses were occupied by such persons as the Revd R. L. Hopper, a surgeon, Captain Blond, a dentist, and Madame Provost -names to speculate over.

Perhaps most interestingly, in 1932 No 1 became Cheltenham's All-Electric Demonstration House, when every room displayed the latest appliances: a breakfast cooker and table griller in the dining room; curling tongs and hair dryer in the bedroom; suction sweeper in the hall; and intriguingly a Health Motor in the bathroom. Even the lounge had its 'Ozonair'. No wonder visitors, from the Mayor downwards, thronged to see these wonders of modern living, especially as the 'bus fare from North Street to Pittville Gates was only a penny.

BOISRAGON, HENRY CHARLES

'I am disordered by the Waters and diluted to the throat with medicine for the stone by Dr Boisragon' wrote Lord Byron from Cheltenham in 1812. This doctor, perhaps one of the most memorable of the time, lived at 11 **Royal Crescent**. His attendance on the Royal Family had earned him the title of Physician Extraordinary to the King, while the town's fashionable patients brought him a yearly income of £3,000. But he was also a man of wider interests, being one of the prominent Masons, a fervent Liberal, and a leading figure in the Literary Society formed by Dr Edward **Jenner**. He became an advocate of aeronautics in the form of ballooning, and as befitted his French ancestry an admirer of King Louis Philippe. At his death in 1852 at Bideford it was acknowledged that despite a lifetime of success he had experienced disappointment as much.

Henry Charles Boisragon's sons too achieved success, in the arts: Theodore was a string player, who on more than one occasion argued for Cheltenham to have its own public orchestra; while Conrad appeared at Covent Garden as a singer.

BOOTH'S AMUSEMENT CENTRE
Although its present use, and its location in the **High Street** amongst modern shops, is misleading, the oddity of this building in shape and character must indicate a history longer than many of its neighbours. In fact it dates back to the early years of the 19th century. Here one of the first **guide books** to Cheltenham, 'Ruff's', written by Thomas Frognal Dibdin, was published in 1803, and in 1809 it saw the beginning of one of the important **newspapers,** the *Cheltenham Chronicle.*

Its subsequent uses were somewhat less impressive, being that of a pastry cook's, a jeans shop and now a self-explanatory 'Amusement' centre.

BRANDON HOUSE
One of Cheltenham's most impressive examples of a town house, it stands near the church of St Philip and St James, **Leckhampton**, at the corner of Painswick and Grafton Roads. Its porch alone is worth studying with its columns having crisply carved classical capitals, and the stonework above bearing beribboned wreaths. The windows on the ground floor are narrower at their top, echoing ancient Egyptian temple entrances.

Brandon House was built about 1825 for Henry Norwood Trye, its long garden stretching all the way along Painswick Road to the appropriately named Tryes Road. These grounds with fine trees and lawns were to prove admirable for pupils when there was a school here. In 1936 an auction brochure suggested that this was land suitable for housing development, though despite the property failing to sell four years later even at a reduced figure of £3,000, subsequent purchasers made sure the idea was taken up. Today houses fill where once were gardens.

Thankfully, Brandon House itself escaped unscathed, and after being an engineering firm's office it is now the headquarters of a builders. Inside the stairs and rooms still recall its past, a time when the house was home within the space of ten years to the Countess of Ponthieu, Archbishop Whately of Dublin, and Admiral MacKellar!

BREWERIES
It was John Gardner, a banker, who started a brewhouse in 1760 on a site in the **High Street** still used for the purpose by Whitbreads. At his death the brewery and his name passed to his brother-in-law, a retired military engineer called James Agg, who thereupon called himself Agg-Gardner; after his death the concern was left to his son James Tynte Agg-Gardner, aged 12 years in 1858. It was not until 1888 that the brewing firm was registered as a company, taking the name Cheltenham Original Brewery.

Despite a disastrous fire in 1897 the trade prospered, as is evidenced by the massive buildings dating from that time which can be seen along Henrietta Street.

During the ensuing years many local takeovers were made, resulting in the formation in 1958 of West Country Breweries Ltd controlling some 1,300 tied houses. Then in 1963 a further acquisition saw Whitbreads now the owner.

Of the other breweries little evidence remains, though in Winchcombe Street, just at the Albion Street crossroads, Warwick Place still shows the last traces of Mr Pointer's establishment, with the wide arch, name panel and fine fanlight surviving.

BUTLER, JOSEPHINE

She was born at Dilston, Northumberland in 1828, of a father who was a radical agricultural reformer, and a mother who was a devout Moravian Christian, so it is hardly surprising that Josephine Butler should become an ardent campaigner for social justice.

Nevertheless that mission was not immediately evident when in 1852 she married George Butler, a lecturer at Durham University. Indeed it was not until the family moved to Cheltenham on his appointment as Vice Principal of **Cheltenham College** in 1857 that the spark was produced, and that through personal tragedy. For in 1864 their 5 year old daughter Eva died in a fall. Josephine recorded 'I became possessed with an irresistible desire to go forth and find some pain greater than mine own'. Her opportunity came when they moved to Liverpool in 1866, for she espoused the destitute and ill prostitutes in the Bridewell, fought tirelessly against the double standards and hypocrisy of the Contagious Diseases Acts and promoted women's education. After being widowed in 1890 she returned from Winchester where George had been a canon residentiary of the cathedral to her native Northumberland.

Whilst in Cheltenham her homes had been, first 26 Priory Street, next to the house Adam Lindsay **Gordon** had lived in as a boy, and then, after three years, a larger residence called The Priory at the corner of London Road, which was the scene of her daughter's tragic death. The former still stands, but the latter, after serving subsequently as a hostel for men students of St Paul's Teacher Training College, was demolished to make room for an office block, Mercian House, where a commemorative plaque recalls Josephine Butler's residence there.

CAMBRAY

One of the most unusual of all Cheltenham's street names, Cambray is probably a family name, originally French. It was given to a field on the south side of the **High Street**, owned in the early years of the 19th century by Joseph **Pitt**. From about 1802 onwards, Cambray Meadow was developed for building, including detached and terraced houses, shops, a bank and a new Theatre Royal. Although many of its original buildings have gone, the houses of about 1820 in Cambray Place are particularly attractive, forming as they do a marked contrast to the Italianate **Cambray Chapel** of 1853-5.

The name Cambray was also applied to one of the town's smaller spa wells, which had the distinction of being a chalybeate (that is, iron-based) spring rather than a saline spring as at the **Royal Well**. First established in 1807 at what was known as Fowler's Cottage, it was replaced in 1834 by a very striking octagonal pump room at the corner of Oriel Road and Rodney Road, near Imperial Square. This building remained in use until 1873, when it became a turkish bath, and it was finally demolished in 1938. Its site is now included in a car park.

CAMBRAY BAPTIST CHAPEL

In Cambray Place is the least altered of all the town's Regency and Victorian chapels, retaining a fine and well-maintained interior.

The chapel was built in the Italianate style in 1853-5 and was designed by the Borough Surveyor, Henry Dangerfield. Its congregation had seceded from **Salem Chapel** in 1843 and met in temporary premises until enough money could be raised to build a purpose-built chapel, which is still in active use today.

At the rear of the chapel is a small school room, and a narrow passage runs alongside the chapel, connecting Cambray Place and Rodney Road.

CARYATIDS

In Montpellier Walk there are 32 figures of armless ladies supporting on their heads the lintels of shop fronts. Based on the classical models at the Erechtheion in Athens they have given this area of **Montpellier** a charming character. Only two of them are original in the sense of being the work of a London sculptor called Rossi. They date from 1840 and are made of terracotta. The remainder were done by a local man from Tivoli Street or have been added as recently as the two concrete examples on the extension of the bank. They were put there only in 1970.

Careful scrutiny of them will reveal that their design is not merely repetitive for some have the right knee forward, others the left.

CAVENDISH HOUSE

Cheltenham's oldest and leading Department Store was established in 1826 when Thomas Clark and William Debenham opened a branch of their London draper's business, which was in Wigmore Street, near Cavendish Square. The new Cheltenham business boasted 'a choice selection of silks, muslins, shawls, handkerchiefs, gauzes, ribands, gloves, lace, hose and fancy articles of English and foreign manufacture'. Its establishment was of great significance, both for Cheltenham's future reputation as a leading

Whitbread Flowers
brewery

No 11 Royal Crescent

Booth's Amusement
Arcade, High Street

shopping centre, particularly for clothing, and for the gradual transformation of the **Promenade** from a residential to a commercial street. Clark and Debenham's, as it was initially known, was the first of the Promenade's shops, and within 15 years most of the houses known as Promenade Villas were also in commercial use.

The history of the store since 1826 has been one of changing ownership and gradual expansion, as its premises were extended to adjoining properties. Although unofficially known as 'Cavendish House' from its early days, that name was officially adopted in 1883, and in 1970 the store became part of the House of Fraser group.

The original store had a fine early 19th century facade which is a prominent feature in many prints and photographs of the Promenade. Sadly, the march of 'progress' led to its removal in 1964-6 and its replacement by the present facade which - despite the store's high quality window displays - does far less for the street-scape than its predecessor had done.

CHARLTON KINGS

To the east of Cheltenham, straddling the main London Road and until 1974 a separate District Council, is Charlton Kings. Like Cheltenham, Charlton has a history dating back to Saxon times, and it still retains its separate identity and atmosphere.

The medieval church stands at the heart of the village, with a number of attractive houses and pubs nearby. Closer to Cheltenham, at the junction of the roads to London and Cirencester, is its second church, Holy Apostles. Designed by John **Middleton**, it was built in 1866-71 to serve the growing population of the area where Cheltenham and Charlton adjoined one another: at this time Charlton parish extended as far west as the present Hales Road (created in 1847 by the widening of Coltham Lane), and included a number of attractive early 19th century artisan streets in Coltham Fields, such as Upper Park Street and Rosehill Street, adjoining an area of former brick fields.

On slightly higher ground, but historically still part of Charlton parish, is the spacious Battledown Estate, laid out from 1860 onwards and containing some of Cheltenham's finest late Victorian houses.

CHELT, RIVER

The small, often culverted, stream that runs through Cheltenham was once a very much more important part of the town's life than it is today. For it was along this stream that the various medieval **mills** which formed the basis of the town's early economy were established. At that time, the stream probably did not have a name, and when it did so, it is believed to have been known as the 'Arle Stream'. The name 'Chelt' is almost certainly later, and is derived from the name of the town rather than vice versa. Exactly what

'Cheltenham' means has long been disputed, but the name is probably derived from two Saxon words, *chilt* (meaning cliff) and *ham* (meaning settlement) - which fits with the town's location under the brow of the Cotswolds.

Although culverted in the town centre, the river may be seen on the east and west sides of the town, and parts of it have been laid out as a recreational area known as the 'Chelt Walk'. It is a particularly attractive feature where it runs through Sandford Park on the east side of the town. In all, the river runs for 11 miles, rising on the Cotswold scarp east of the Dowdeswell reservoir, and emptying into the Severn between Gloucester and Tewkesbury.

CHELTENHAM AND GLOUCESTER BUILDING SOCIETY

As a building society which the town can claim as its own, the 'C & G', as it is widely known, deserves acknowledgment here. In 1850 a meeting was held in the Belle Vue Hotel, an establishment run by Mr Benjamin Thomas, who was also a wine merchant and auctioneer. The building, in London Road, still stands though converted into flats. Originally it was the town house of the Hicks-Beach family, and here Lewis Carroll stayed in 1863 whilst the Liddells were at Hetton Lawn in **Charlton Kings**.

If one person is to be named as the moving figure in founding the society then it must be James Downing, a draper in the **High Street**. By the time he died in 1868, the success of the enterprise was assured.

The main office of the society was in **Clarence Street**, only vacating its purpose-built accommodation in 1990. On its facade there is still a composition dating from 1972 by the eminent sculptor Barbara Hepworth.

CHELTENHAM AND GLOUCESTER COLLEGE OF HIGHER EDUCATION

Established in 1990 by amalgamation, its history and buildings owe much to the former teachers' training colleges of St Paul's and St Mary's. It was largely due to the energetic personality of Francis **Close** and the initial generosity of a local resident, Miss Jane Cook, in providing a 5-acre site, that the Normal College as it was first called was located in the **St Paul's** area of the town. On 19 April 1849 the Earl of Shaftesbury laid the foundation stone of the Oxford-style college building designed by S.W.**Daukes**. Today its medieval front and quadrangle tower are appreciated for their Victorian emphasis on the visual appropriateness of Gothic as an expression of the academic and devotional life. For St Paul's College was to be on 'scriptural, evangelical and Protestant principles in accordance with the Established Church'. Interestingly the chapel was not built until 1909, and even then was not aligned on the customary east-west axis.

Cavendish House

Brandon House

Charlton Kings: Hetton
Lawn and Box Cottage

One of the caryatids between shops
in Montpellier Walk

As well as Francis Close Hall as it is now called, the College has other sites. In **St George's Place** stands Shaftesbury Hall, opened in 1869 as St Mary's Hall to accommodate women students of the training college. The red brick building was described as being one of the cheapest of its kind in the country. Strangely there is no foundation stone but it is known that a local architect, J.T.Darby won the commission after an open competition.

The nearby **Quaker** House was built in 1835, costing the Society of Friends a mere £1,200. The College acquired it in 1902.

In **The Park** there are a number of substantial mansions and villas owned by the College, while on the northern edge of town Rosehill had a significant history in that it is recorded that in 1824 J.B.**Papworth** came here to make a preliminary survey for a house. How much the property owed to his design is not clear, but a richly decorated main room with rococo walls and painted ceiling was certainly memorable, before all was demolished in 1992 to make way for the offices of Gulf Oil.

CHELTENHAM CHAPEL

Cheltenham's earliest surviving Nonconformist Chapel stands on one side of the bowling green in **St George's Square** off Lower High Street. Built in 1808-9 in response to the lack of space in the town's existing church and chapels, its promoter was the well-known Nonconformist minister, the Revd Rowland Hill of Surrey Chapel, Blackfriars, who had strong Gloucestershire connections.

The former chapel is built of brick with a stuccoed facade bearing the name and date of the building, and it retains its cast-iron interior gallery structure. The building was designed by a local architect named Edward Smith. From the time of its opening in August 1809 until the middle of the century, the chapel was a major focus of religious life in the town, and played an important part in the growth of religious fervour that gave the town its distinctive Victorian character. It was later used by Congregationalists, Presbyterians and the Salvation Army, before serving for some years (somewhat ironically, given its previous use) as a wine warehouse, before its recent and very successful conversion for office accommodation. The conversion included the demolition of a small Sunday School wing at the rear of the building, and its replacement by a neat octagonal extension.

Adjoining the chapel is a small graveyard, opened in 1810. It too has been cleared and restored in recent years, and is a pleasant oasis in a busy part of the town.

CHELTENHAM COLLEGE

It has a claim to be called the first Victorian Public School, for it dates from 1841. Founded on the Proprietary system whereby shareholders had the right to nominate pupils, the school owed much to the support of Francis Close. From its beginnings the teaching was divided into Classical and what was called Military departments. As might be expected therefore many boys were prepared for the army, indeed the school can boast that it has the greatest number of Victoria Cross recipients amongst its past pupils. Other distinguished Old Cheltonians include Adam Lindsay **Gordon**, Australia's poet, F.H.Bradley the philosopher, Edward **Wilson** the Antarctic explorer, Glubb Pasha of the Arab Legion and J.Dykes-Bower, organist of St Paul's Cathedral for 31 years.

Architecturally the College is a varied assortment. The main building dressed out in 15th century Gothic style with a central tower dates from the first years of the school's existence, and was designed by James Wilson from Bath. Beside its long facade facing Bath Road rises on its own the chapel, built in 1896 in the King's College, Cambridge, idiom. The interior has a fine carved reredos to the altar, the work of the local firm, Boultons, and a particularly refined example of wood carving is to be found on the south wall panelling, carved by **H.H.Martyn & Co.**

At the south side of the main building, across the road is Thirlestaine House. Started in 1823 to the design of its owner, J.R.Scott, who spent some £80,000 on it, this magnificent example of classical portico, with carvings copied from the Parthenon in Athens was enlarged by the next owner, Lord Northwick, to provide space for displaying his collection of 1,500 paintings. But perhaps it was the next occupant, the legendary bibliophile Sir Thomas Phillipps who most needed storage room, for he amassed some 100,000 books and 60,000 manuscripts.

In 1947 the College purchased the house for £31,326, not bad for a mansion once considered as a suitable residence for a king - William IV.

CHELTENHAM LADIES' COLLEGE

In the autumn of 1853 six men including the Principal and Vice-Principal of the Boys' College met to consider the possibility of doing something in the town for the better education of girls. They resolved 'that an institution for the daughters and young children of Noblemen and Gentlemen be established'. Shares of £10 were to be issued, entitling the owner of each to nominate one pupil.

The site of the first building was where Cambray Court flats now stand, and it served the school for 20 years. Soon the Presidency of the school's Council was offered to the Revd Francis **Close**, and the first Lady Principal appointed. However, with the former's move to become Dean of Carlisle and the resignation of the latter in 1857, the school's future appeared uncertain.

Then in 1858 Dorothea **Beale**, aged 27, was made Principal. By 1873 the present site was occupied, though at the cost of destroying the **Well**

Cheltenham College

Francis Close Hall, Cheltenham & Gloucester College of Higher Education

Former Wesleyan chapel, St George's Street, and Highbury chapel, Grosvenor Street

Figures on the Odeon cinema façade

Cheltenham Ladies' College

Walk where **George III** had taken the waters. The new building had further additions by John **Middleton** who in 1876 erected the French-looking tower. From then on the frontage to Montpellier Street rapidly filled, perhaps the most conspicuous part being the Princess Hall of 1897. This was a replacement for the old Theatre Royal which had been such a feature in Cheltenham's development.

Expansion under the inspired leadership of Miss Beale, and her successors after 1906, has seen the filling of the area bounded by Bayshill Road, Fauconberg Road and St George's Road. The style has varied: sometimes it is Cotswold vernacular, other times it is 1950s modern. Fortunately there has also been preservation of existing buildings, as in the cases of the impressive Fauconberg House, built in 1847, with its fine classical details particularly in the cast iron gate piers, and the four villas in Bayshill Road, all designed by Samuel Onley.

Having been a boarding school since its foundation, the Ladies' College possesses a number of important houses in the area. Notable examples of past and present ones include Sidney Lodge, the previous home of **Baron de Ferrieres**, Montpellier House in **Suffolk Square**, where Sir Robert **Smirke** lived, and the Savoy Hotel in Bayshill Road.

CHRISTADELPHIAN HALL

The Christadelphian Hall in Knapp Road was originally the Bethel Baptist Chapel, built in 1820 to replace a smaller chapel of 1701-2 on the same site. Architecturally, the building is typical of its date, being the epitome of what has been termed a 'dissenters' box'. It is built of brick, with an ashlar stone facade, and has a well-cared for graveyard and garden on one side.

CHRIST CHURCH

Like **St Gregory's** RC Church, Christ Church makes a dramatic focus to its road. Even from more distant places its tower presents almost cathedral majesty. Yet not all descriptions have been favourable: ' a Staffordshire china ornament that could stand on the largest chimney piece in the world.... a tall Perpendicularish tower with a lamentable expression; you expect it to sob'. Admittedly after the gigantic scale of its 'west' end - that in fact faces south - the rest of the church somewhat fades into an insignificant apse. But then in fairness, the **Jearrad**s, the original architects in 1836, have had their design of a straightforward 'preaching box' considerably altered. In 1888 J.**Middleton** added the domed apse, wall decoration by Sir William Richmond and J.E.Reid followed, and much marble embellishment has turned the interior into something from Italy. Nevertheless, there are survivors from the early years: notice boards inside the tower entrance decree that 'Chairs are not allowed to take up at this door or stand in any part of the carriageway', and 'Day tickets may be obtained admitting to all the services of the day at 1s 6d. The doorkeepers and pew openers are strictly prohibited from receiving money as fees'. Predictably the memorials reflect Cheltenham's association with India, but some commemorate the Gaitskill family, and one, Gordon of Khartoum.

When all's said and done, it is the tower that makes Christ Church.

CHURCHES AND CHAPELS

Cheltenham's only medieval church is **St Mary's**, but the rapid expansion of the town in the early 19th century resulted in a number of additional places of worship for the Established Church being built, not only for the genteel but also artisan classes. In the case of the former, seating was subscribed for; the latter had it free. Surprisingly in such a Regency environment, only one church, **St Paul's**, is classical in style, though another, **St John's**, was built only to be demolished a few years ago. Of the Gothic revival examples **All Saints, Christ Church, Holy Trinity, St Mark's** and **St Matthew's** are notable. **St Peter's** provides a fine Norman revival essay, while **St James'** is no longer used for worship. Of the Roman Catholic churches **St Gregory's** is outstanding, not least in its contribution to the 'steeplescape' of Cheltenham.

Cheltenham is also fortunate in that no less than 13 Nonconformist chapels and meeting houses survive from the years 1808-55, although only about half are now used for worship. Like the Anglican churches, the chapels display a wide range of architectural styles - from the simple box-like structures of the very early 19th century, such as the **Christadelphian Hall**, to the elaborate Gothic revival **Salem Chapel**.

CINEMAS

Of the many cinemas, so popular in the early decades of the century, only one is still active. It stands in Winchcombe Street on the site of the old **Highbury Chapel**, and before that the Albion Livery stables. The first film shown, in March 1933, was 'Rome Express', to an audience filling the 2,000 seats. Not only was there the fine Compton organ, later sold to an Australian concert hall in Melbourne, but many live performances from such stars as Harry Worth, Tommy Steele, the Goons, Dick Emery, the Beverley Sisters and the Beatles. Outside over the foyer canopy are two dancing ladies seemingly for ever trying to sort out swirling twists of film lengths. Apparently they were intended to typify the spirit and romance of the silver screen, being the work of Newbury Trent, cousin of the cinema's architect.

One other building in the town still proclaims its ancestry even though it is no longer a cinema. It is to be found in Suffolk Parade and has little changed since it opened in October 1922 with a Thunderclap - the film of course. Above the chequer tiled entrance and box office the name 'Daffodil' announces itself, and even now in the auditorium the proscenium fittings remain. Only a few years ago the projection room was rediscovered still fully equipped.

Finally, **Royscot House** at the southern end of the **Promenade** terrace remembers that its immediate predecessor was a cinema, for it displays in the modern building three decorative roundels saved from the interior of that place. Their subjects are classical figures including a centaur and victory, being executed by the noted Cheltenham firm of **H.H.Martyn & Co.**

CLAREMONT LODGE

For many admirers of Regency architecture, Claremont Lodge, standing at the junction of Vittoria Walk with Montpellier Spa Road, comes high in their selection of houses. Its front facing east has all the characteristics of the era: a graceful balcony curving round the bow, elegantly enriching its proportions. At the side an entrance door, flanked by classical columns and bootscrapers, has above it the whirls of a fanlight, and to each side along the wall four circular 'porthole' windows lead in their turn to more classical details of columns, niches and urns. Even the pavement outside the doorway has been given strips of darker stone.

Not surprisingly, there have been distinguished occupants: in 1837 Sir William Baginall Burdett, in 1845 the Revd Sir Nicholas Chinnery, and in 1867 Lady Combermere. From 1919 to 1927 Dr James Clay Shaw lived here, an authority on insanity and psychological medicine at London's St Bartholomew's Hospital. However he was also a little eccentric himself, being of the opinion that 'modern woman's' activity in sport would 'mar the beauty of her face, change her nature and alienate male sympathy'.

Interestingly, the house was not built all of a piece. The top floor, for instance, was added later; and that masterly street front came into being only when a small courtyard was enclosed. The original front door with another delightful fanlight still exists behind, while classical columns in some cases protrude into rooms. Most intriguing of all, there is over a fireplace, painted actually in the plaster, a depiction of the house as it was before the alterations.

CLARENCE SQUARE

Part of the **Pittville Estate**, the Square was laid out in the late 1820s, although its earliest houses were not built until 1832. On three sides are attractive stuccoed terraces in a traditional classical style, many of them with particularly fine examples of ornamental ironwork, especially the many cast iron bootscrapers by the doors. By way of a contrast, the fourth side has a restrained Gothic Revival terrace, dating from 1840-44. The Square was named after the Duke of Clarence, who became King William

IV in 1830; among its notable residents was Charles **Sturt**, who lived at No 19 between 1863 and 1869.

Running out of Clarence Sqare to the east is Clarence Road (formerly Pittville Terrace), with houses of a similar date and style to those in the Square. Of them, two merit particular attention -**Billbrook House**, at the corner of Winchcombe Street, and 4 Clarence Road, the birthplace, in 1874, of the composer Gustav **Holst**.

Before the development of Pittville, part of the site of Clarence Square (its south-east corner) was occupied by a farmhouse called Field Lodge or Arkell's Farm. It was here, in 1803, that the great actress, Sarah Siddons, who had been 'discovered' in Cheltenham's playhouse many years earlier, lived for a time. She described it as 'a little cottage ..... some distance from the town, perfectly retired, surrounded by hills and fields and groves'.

CLARENCE STREET

One of central Cheltenham's principal thoroughfares, it contains a number of buildings of interest, notably the **Public Library, Art Gallery and Museum**, and the former headquarters of the **Cheltenham and Gloucester Building Society**. It has only, however, been known as Clarence Street since 1827, when Adelaide, Duchess of Clarence (later Queen Adelaide, wife of William IV) drove in her carriage along the newly-created street on her way to stay at Liddell's Boarding House, subsequently renamed the Clarence Hotel, and now **John Dower House**.

Before 1827, Clarence Street was a narrower roadway known as 'the Great House Road', after the early 18th century 'Great House' that stood on the site of **St Matthew's Church**. Originally the residence of Lady Stapleton, the Great House became the town's leading boarding house in the latter part of the 18th century, and was eventually incorporated into the Clarence Hotel; it was demolished in 1853.

CLOSE, REVEREND FRANCIS

'The great man of the place, monarch of all he surveys.....never did Beau Nash rule with more absolute supremacy. The authorities of the town sink into insignificance when their influence is placed beside that of the potent vicar.' Such an estimate is borne out by the example alone of the sermon he preached, and that when he had been only a year as incumbent of **St Mary's**. It was on the evils of **horse-racing**, a subject to which he returned many times. Within four days of his delivering it, over 3,500 copies were sold.

Born in 1797 at Frome in Somerset, Francis Close came to Cheltenham in 1824 as curate to **Holy Trinity** Church. Two years later he accepted the living of St Mary's, thus beginning a 'reign' which ended in 1856 on his being appointed Dean of Carlisle. His strong views on racing were not the

Revd Francis Close

Former Daffodil cinema

Claremont Lodge

only ones he voiced. The **theatres** too came under his scathing tongue, with alcohol, tobacco and indeed **railways**, particularly Sunday trains. As another observer commented, 'The Sabbath is better kept in Cheltenham than anywhere else outside Scotland.'

Politically, Close was Conservative, implacably opposed to the Liberal **Berkeleys**, and in Churchmanship wholly an Evangelical, viewing High practices with abhorrence.

Perhaps his most memorable cause was that of education. He was instrumental in the building of some five churches with their schools; to him as much as **Wilderspin, St James's Square Infants' School** owed its inception; **Cheltenham College** and the **Ladies' College**, the two training colleges of St Paul and St Mary, now part of the **Cheltenham and Gloucester College of Higher Education**, can all look to him as a founding father, while **Dean Close School**, though established after his death, perpetuates his memory.

Tennyson's description of him as 'the Pope of Cheltenham' disguises the immense support he enjoyed not only in the large congregations but also throughout the town and further afield.

COLLEGE BATHS
Considered by the Victorian Society to be the oldest swimming pool surviving intact in the country, the interior of the building, standing appropriately in College Baths Road, seems to be unchanged. Built to the design of W.H.Knight, it was opened around 1880. There are the original cubicles, even cast iron coat hooks and delightful decorative floral tiles. The external appearance too has remained much as it was, with a majestic Wellingtonia tree and the Poolkeeper's house still standing.

COLLEDGE, THOMAS RICHARDSON
Founder and first president of the Medical Missionary Society in China, Dr Thomas Richardson Colledge (1796-1879) spent the last 38 years of his life in Cheltenham. He lived and died at Lauriston House in **Montpellier**, a fine building dating from 1840, whose classical style includes a porch with capitals copied from the Tower of the Winds in Athens. The house probably takes its name from a district in Edinburgh with which Colledge had associations.

COLLEGES
There is a need to make the distinction clear that there are in the town educational establishments which call themselves colleges but are schools, and others which come into the category of tertiary colleges. For the former, **Cheltenham College** and the **Ladies' College**, and the latter **Cheltenham and Gloucester College of Higher Education** serve as examples.

COLUMBIA PLACE

The name of this striking terrace of six houses in Winchcombe Street, near the Pittville Gates (now 112-122 Winchcombe Street), recalls an unexpected link between Cheltenham and South America. The houses, which date from 1824-5, were built by a former Army saddler named Thomas Thompson, who had made his fortune supplying cavalry equipment to various South American states. Among these was Columbia (now Colombia), where he had also obtained from its leader, General Bolivar, a monopoly for the refining and sale of salt from the country's various salt mines.

Whilst on a visit to Cheltenham to drink the waters, Thompson decided to invest a part of his fortune in the building of the terrace, which would then be let out aslodgings for visitors. To design it, he employed an architect who also had American connections, William **Jay,** who had only recently returned to England after several years at Savannah, in Georgia, where he had designed a large number of houses. Jay's terrace is most unusual in its style, and has particularly attractive ironwork.

The use of the name Columbia was not lost on contemporaries, William Cobbett, visiting Cheltenham in 1826, derided the name, saying that it must have been given to it 'by some dealer in bonds', and it is an added irony that the building boom of 1822-25 which no doubt prompted Thompson to build his houses was brought to a sudden end in December 1825 by a financial crisis involving over-speculation in dubious South American mining shares!

Interestingly, there is also another 'Columbia' not far from Columbia Place: one of the small streets of **Fairview** is called Columbia Street, although in its early days it was known as Philadelphia Street. In this instance, however, the reason for the choice of name is not known.

COOMBE HILL CANAL

Although not actually in Cheltenham itself, the now disused and overgrown Coombe Hill Canal, which had its wharves at Coombe Hill, five miles west of Cheltenham, played an important part in Cheltenham's development between its opening in 1796 and the establishment of the Cheltenham and Gloucester tramroad in 1811. For it was along this canal that much of the building materials and fuel required by the town was brought, particularly Forest stone, coal, timber and ironwork. The canal gave Cheltenham access to Gloucester Docks and the River Severn (which it joined at Wainlodes, three miles west of Coombe Hill), the remainder of the journey to Cheltenham being made by road. The canal remained open, albeit not much used, until 1876, and it is now an attractive nature reserve.

CORALS SNOOKER HALL, ALBION STREET

One of Cheltenham's variety theatres, this building was opened by Cecil Gillsmith as the Hippodrome in 1913. Many famous names in the music hall tradition appeared on its stage: Will Hay, Harry Tate, Billy Danvers and Randolph Sutton among them. The then-unknown Gracie Fields too came in 1916. There is a story that the song 'It's a long, long way to Tipperary' was composed in No. 1 dressing room by Jack Judge, and indeed performed for the first time here.

In 1919 a Mr H.G.Beard from Gloucester bought the place, renaming it the Coliseum. Then in 1931, it became a cinema.

CRICKET

The first class game has been played here since 1872 when James Lillywhite, cricket coach at **Cheltenham College**, suggested that during the summer holiday a match should be held on its ground. He was given £10 and told to arrange everything. Clearly he did the job well, helped no doubt by the exploits of the county captain, W.G.Grace, who, in the 1874 match, took 7 wickets for 7 runs in the first innings and 7 for 18 in the second, and who, in the 1876 match, scored 318 not out.

By 1878 a second match was introduced, thereby constituting a 'Cricket Week', for which Lillywhite was allocated £120, while in 1906 the addition of a third fixture elevated the event to a 'Cricket Festival'.

There has been exciting play on this ground: in that 1906 local 'Derby' against Worcestershire the visitors could make only 147 and 146 in reply to the home side's 523, and 29 years later Gloucestershire savoured a moment of glory when it beat the South African touring side by 87 runs, W.R.Hammond scoring 123 and R.Sinfield 102 as well as taking 5 wickets for 31 runs.

Cheltenham-born G.L.**Jessop** took 4 for 9 runs against Yorkshire in 1895, and his fast scoring included 33 in 13 minutes against Kent, and 53 in 15 minutes against Hampshire's attack. More recently Zaheer in 1977 made 205 not out and 108 in the Sussex match, while in 1979 M.Procter humbled Yorkshire with a hat-trick of lbw's, thus echoing on this ground the Somerset match of 1893 when for the only time in the history of the first class game a hat-trick of stumpings was achieved by the home side.

All these momentous happenings have taken place in a setting unequalled, some might say, in the world of cricket grounds: green grass, white tents, majestic school buildings.

DARLING, SIR RALPH

By all accounts, Sir Ralph Darling was not an attractive personality. A strict disciplinarian, painfully precise, sternly reserved and a stickler for petty details, he became Governor of New South Wales in 1825. It was during his tenure of the post that much exploration of Australia took place, principally by Charles **Sturt** who served for a time as his military secretary. It is for this reason that Darling's name appears more than any other governor's on the map, for example the river and mountain range. A parliamentary select committee was appointed to enquire into his conduct as governor, particularly in the matter of cruelty to convicted soldiers, and the granting of Crown lands. Although Darling was judged free from blame, it must have been common knowledge when he came to live at 7, Lansdown Terrace in Cheltenham. Maybe the fact that not only he but his two brothers were generals admitted him to the town's society. However he did not spend all of his remaining years here, for he died in 1858 at Brighton. The house later became the residence of the Revd Thomas **Mozley**, and to the town came also Charles Sturt.

DAUKES, SAMUEL WHITFIELD
The son of a businessman trading in mining and brewing, being descended from the French family d'Aux, Samuel Whitfield Daukes was born in London in 1811. He trained under J.P.Pritchett of York, thereby bringing him into contact with John **Middleton**. Indeed it was Daukes who persuaded his fellow student to join him in Cheltenham. In 1839, following Thomas Billings' unsuccessful enterprise, Daukes bought **The Park**, developing it to include his own house Tudor Lodge, now only a name surviving on street signs.

In Cheltenham his work can, however, still be seen with such varying examples as the railway station at **Lansdown, St Peter's Church**, Tewkesbury Road, and most conspicuously Francis Close Hall at the **Cheltenham and Gloucester College of Higher Education**.

But he did not confine his activities to the town, being architect from 1839 to 1842 to the Birmingham and Gloucester Railway, designer of the Royal Agricultural College, Cirencester, and churches such as St Saviour's at Tetbury. He also remodelled Witley Court in Worcestershire.

He died at Beckenham in Kent in 1880 and was buried in the family vault at Highgate Cemetery. Incidentally, two of his grandsons became a bishop and a knight.

DAY LEWIS, CECIL
The son of a Church of Ireland minister, Cecil Day Lewis was born in that country in 1904, coming to England the following year. Educated at Sherborne School and Oxford University he became a master at **Cheltenham College** Junior School in 1930. For a year he rented Belmore House, at 96 Bath Road, before moving to an older property, the brick and Cotswold stone Box Cottage at Bafford Lane in **Charlton Kings**. During his stay of seven years the roof needed attention, and to help pay for it he

Clarence
Square

Columbia Place

the Cricket Festival
on Cheltenham College
Ground

decided to become a writer of detective stories. In 1935 there appeared the first of some 20 thrillers by 'Nicholas Blake' featuring the resourceful sleuth Nigel Strangeways. It was called *A Question of Proof*, and its reception by the College authorities was less warm than that by the general readers. In the event his use of the thinly-disguised setting of the school led to his resignation and in 1938 he moved to Devon. Subsequently Professor of Poetry at Oxford from 1951 to 1956, he was appointed Poet Laureate in 1968, and died in 1972. His widow, actress Jill Balcon, unveiled a plaque commemorating his years at Box Cottage.

DE FERRIERES, BARON

Born in Utrecht in 1809, the third Baron Charles Conrad Adolphus du Bois Ferrieres came from a distinguished family. His grandfather, Col du Bois, commander of the Dutch Cavalry Guards, was made a General by Napoleon. After early years in Chepstow, Charles moved with his family to Dee, near Chester, and in 1860 to Cheltenham. Seven years later he became naturalised.

His involvement in the affairs of the town and his benefactions to its churches, schools and cultural resources were notable. One of the first aldermen to be elected in 1876, he was made the Borough's second Mayor the following year, and was returned to Parliament as its Member in 1880.

But perhaps his most memorable gesture was the gift of 43 pictures from his father's collection of 17th century Dutch and 19th century Belgian work, together with £1,000 towards the building of an **Art Gallery** for the town.

His house in Overton Road, with its extraordinary stonework, is now called Sidney Lodge. It stands on the site once occupied by Lord Fauconberg's Bayshill House where that other, more indirect, benefactor of Cheltenham, **George III**, stayed.

DEAN CLOSE SCHOOL

Four years after the death of Francis **Close** in 1882, it was decided that 'the most fitting memorial would be a middle class school' providing an education 'based on the scriptural and evangelical principles of the Church of England'. A subscription list was opened and £10,000 was provided to endow the Dean Close Memorial School.

Its main buildings in Shelburne Road are of sombre red brick tricked out with Dutch gables. They date from 1886, but the chapel did not appear until 1923.

Of the accomplishments of past pupils perhaps the most well known were those of James Elroy Flecker, son of a Headmaster, whose *Hassan* is complemented by poems centred on his memories of days at school. *November Eves* includes references to the appearance of **Leckhampton** Hill during a Cheltenham winter.

DEVONSHIRE STREET SCHOOL

Of the ordinary schools in the town, as distinct from the private institutions, no better example can be described than that in Devonshire Street. Its Gothic style windows may not have the splendour of those in the large public schools, but it can boast a pedigree longer than they.

For it was the direct successor of a school established in 1683 over the north porch of **St Mary's Church**. Thanks to the support of Francis **Close** it did not disappear when National Schools began but found a new location just off the **High Street**. Perhaps the pupils missed the churchyard which served as their playground, or having to manhandle their aged headmaster, John Garn, up the steep stairs to the classroom.

Today it is no longer a school, though on the wall there is still a poignant War Memorial inscription that reads:

They trod of old the fields we tread,
They played the games we play,
The part of them that is not dead
Belongs to us today.

DIGHTON, RICHARD

Among the many notable artists who lived for a time at Cheltenham was the portrait painter Richard Dighton, who made his living painting small full-figure portraits of many of the town's residents and visitors.

Dighton, who was born in London in 1796, first came to Cheltenham in 1828. He then moved to Worcester for a time, from where he returned to Cheltenham in 1832 for a longer stay of up to eight years. He is recorded as living at a number of addresses, including 67 St George's Place, 7 Promenade Villas and Woodland Cottage, Prestbury Road. He died in London in 1880.

DOBELL, SYDNEY

Born in 1824 at Cranbrook, Kent, Sydney Dobell came to Cheltenham when his father, a wine merchant, set up in premises whose ground floor can still be seen opposite the former **Gas Works** offices at the corner of Lower High Street. Here the 12 year old boy acted as clerk in the counting house, thereby motivating his father to note admiringly, 'He has never yet received any lesson, pursues Latin, French etc by himself at intervals between business....he remembers everything he devours.' Young Sydney certainly attended neither school nor university, yet proved to be a master of language, a kind employer, blameless in character and philanthropic to all. He championed struggling authors, and identified himself in his most notable poem *The Roman* with the aspirations of Italian unity. Thus he received the praise of such revolutionaries as Mazzini and Kossuth as well as celebrities like **Tennyson**, Carlyle, Holman Hunt and Rosetti. It was whilst living at Coxhorne in **Charlton Kings** that he formed the Society of the Friends of Italy.

Ill-health compelled moves to many parts of Britain, Spain, Italy and France, but from 1866 till his death in 1874 he was a Gloucestershire poet, albeit an obscure one. Of his marriage in 1844 it was said that in 30 years he and his wife were never more than 30 hours apart, and something of that ideal permeated his life.

He was buried in Painswick churchyard, almost as if that place of trimmed yews and elegant tombstones fitted his character more than the wine merchant's office. Of his other poems, some may be found in anthologies, but 'Dobells' still has a place in Cheltenham's **Promenade**, even if the name does not appear in the list of Poet Laureates as once was predicted.

DOWTY GROUP

The large organisation, Dowty, has inseparable connections with Cheltenham, firstly because its founder worked nearby and secondly because he happened to be living in the town when he started his own business. There may be a third reason, he was a local person in the sense of being born in Pershore.

After apprenticeship and various posts with engineering firms, George Dowty returned to the west of England, taking a design position in 1924 with the **Gloster Aircraft Company**. Whilst there he developed on his own improvements in undercarriage shock absorbers. But the real success story began in 1931 when he returned from work to his flat in Lansdown Terrace, Malvern Road to find a telegram awaiting him.

It was from the Kawasaki Aircraft Company in Japan asking about the new type of landing wheel Dowty had invented. Soon a firm order for six was placed and as Gloster's were unable to meet the request, Dowty resigned from that company and decided to make the wheels himself. He rented a mews loft in the lane behind his flat, equipped it and set to work.

Despite the neighbouring premises being a petrol store, and the floor below having an abundance of wood shavings, he did not wait for even the formalities of fire insurance! Within two months the order was completed - and the firm of Dowty's had begun its journey to world wide success, not only in the field of aircraft but also in the wider application of hydraulic equipment to such industries as mining.

By 1935 the company had outgrown its premises in Cheltenham's Grosvenor Place South and purchased the estate at **Arle Court**, making the palatial Victorian mansion the springboard for building a vast factory in its 100 acres.

Sidney Lodge, former home of Baron de Ferrieres

Pier at the Park surviving from Tudor Lodge, S.W. Daukes' house

Former Devonshire Street School

DUNALLY HOUSE

In the **St Paul's** area there is one building that seems to be a stranger amongst the artisan terraced houses. For one thing it stands at an angle to the road, and for another its sheer size makes it an oddity. Add to those the mixture of windows and double ridged roof and the place almost cries out for a story.

Originally called Woodbine Cottage, it was renamed North Lodge when the Irish Lord Dunally took it, and eventually, or perhaps inevitably, it ended up being known as Dunally Lodge or House.

But odd as the building may be, what happened nearby, a few years before its erection, is even stranger. In 1777 a body was brought here to be hung in chains, as a dreadful warning of what happened to murderers. However, within a short while both corpse and gibbet had mysteriously disappeared. Some years afterwards when a hedge was being planted at the spot the remains were revealed, so frightening the discoverer that he died a few days later.

As for the crime which caused all this, there is a memorial tablet under the rose window inside **St. Mary's** Church which tells of Katherine a' Court. She came to Cheltenham, lodging in the area with her servant whom she found in the act of stealing. His revenge was to poison her, and his reward was to be sentenced to death himself. The inscription puts it so much better!

EAGLE STAR

From a distance and indeed from many viewpoints in the town the most conspicuous building in Cheltenham must be the office tower of Eagle Star. Its 13 storeys rise to 200ft and although not in fact the tallest structure in the town, the visual impact of such a bulk makes its influence on the streetscape considerable. Officially opened on 18 October 1968 to accommodate the company's administrative head office together with the computer centre, the cost of building was £1.7m. The other cost was what had to be demolished to make space for it: one hotel and two private houses. However, another hotel, the Montpellier, was saved and it is now called Eagle Lodge, restored to its original appearance with pleasant classical porch and decorative shell carving over the windows. A second house, Star Lodge, has also been preserved, but perhaps most important of all, the fine cedar tree on the corner of Bath Road and Montpellier Terrace still stands.

EBENEZER METHODIST CHAPEL

Recently restored for use as flats, and now known as Kings Court, the former Ebenezer Methodist Chapel in King Street adds dignity to one of the narrow streets off the Lower High Street. It was built in 1812-13, as

Coxhorne, Charlton Kings, home of Sydney Dobell

Dunally House

George Dowty's workshop in Lansdown Terrace Lane mews

witnessed by the inscription on its pedimented front. It was constructed of brick and stucco with stone dressings at a total cost of £2,424, and once accommodated 1,000 worshippers. It was later (1839) replaced by a larger chapel in St George's Street (now disused) a little nearer the town centre, and was subsequently occupied by Baptists and Primitive Methodists, before serving for many years as a furniture warehouse. The recent restoration has included the replacement of its Doric style porch, which had been removed many years before, and the renovation of the former Minister's house adjoining the front of the chapel, with a good fanlight.

ELECTRICITY SUB-STATION
One of Cheltenham's most unusual industrial buildings, the terracotta brick electricity sub-station in **Clarence Street** is modelled on the 15th century Palazzo Strozzi in Florence! It was built in 1894-5 as part of the town's first electricity system, and was probably designed by the Borough Engineer, Joseph Hall, who was also responsible for an electricity power plant near Arle Road, to the west of the town centre, and for designing the town's distinctive 'dragon and onion' **street lamps**. Hall, a man of great flair and imagination, later helped to reinforce Cheltenham's links with India, for in 1903 he became Chief Engineer of Bombay.

In 1907, the sub-station was converted for use as the Electricity Company offices, and part of it later served as the Electricity Social Club. Now, however, it has reverted to its former use, its origin having been commemorated by a plaque on the side of the building.

EVERYMAN THEATRE
Originally 'The New Theatre and Opera House', it remains today as one of the best examples of the work of Frank Matcham, the architect who also designed London's Palladium and Coliseum. Built in six months, the frontage to Regent Street belies in its restrained decoration the exuberant carving and glittering detail of the auditorium. Here inside, all is fantasy, with riotous shapes and optical illusion, the flat ceiling for example giving the effect of a dome.

It opened on 1 October 1891 when Lillie Langtry, herself no stranger to Cheltenham, brought her Company down from the Princess's Theatre, London. From then onwards many famous stage personalities appeared here. Ellen Terry, Frank Benson, George Robey, John Gielgud, Margot Fonteyn and Robert Helpmann are but representatives of the varied presentations ranging from ballet to knockabout comedy.

Interestingly, the first showing of a film 'talkie' was here in October 1929 with *Bulldog Drummond* starring Ronald Colman and Joan Bennet. The next week featured Al Jolson in *The Singing Fool*. Indeed until 1936 the theatre was chiefly used to show films, and after a brief heyday during the ensuing war when many London actors gratefully took the opportunity of playing to provincial audiences, the lean years came with the competition from television.

So in 1955 the Borough Council purchased the place and without much success ran it for 18 months. By June 1959 closure came. However, a group of public spirited people formed an Association, found money and negotiated with the Council. Within the year the 'Everyman' had been born, to flourish as Cheltenham's professional theatre throughout the next two decades.

By the 1980s there was evidence that the building needed major restoration, so from 1983 to 1986 much was done in reconstruction and improvement, including a new performance space appropriately named the **Richardson** Studio, in honour of Cheltenham's actor son.

Today the activities are wide ranging: plays, ballet, opera, concerts, training programmes to local communities and schools projects. Truly 'Everyman' has been an apt choice of name.

FAIRVIEW

Fairview, one of Cheltenham's most attractive areas of small early 19th century houses, was developed from about 1806 onwards. Bounded by Winchcombe Street, Albion Street and All Saints Road, Fairview stands on part of the 'Open Fields' to the north of the town, which were 'inclosed' by Act of Parliament in 1806, to enable their development for much- needed building land.

The name Fairview almost certainly derives from the now-demolished Fairview Cottage which stood on the north side of Fairview Road. The site is now occupied by some modern houses to the east of the large red brick All Saints School of 1890, at the corner of Fairview Street. The cottage, which eventually became the Fairview Inn, was the home of a **Charlton Kings** farmer named William Flatcher, who owned much of the adjacent land - clearly, when he lived there in the very early years of the 19th century, his cottage must have commanded a 'fair view' across the fields to the Cotswold Hills.

Gradually, however, Flatcher and a number of other landowners filled up those fields with streets of small artisan houses, to accommodate the large numbers of people who moved to Cheltenham to work in service, the building industry or manufacturing. The latter included coach building, cabinet making and candle making, all of which were carried on in Fairview's many workshops.

Despite the 'slum clearance' of some of the area's poorer housing during the 1930s, many of the original houses remain, and have been restored and renovated under a General Improvement Scheme, sponsored by the Borough Council from 1976 onwards. The earliest houses, dating from

1806-20, are in Gloucester Place and Sherborne Street, but perhaps the most attractive are those of the 1820s, in Fairview Street and in the small streets of 'Coneygree Field', such as York Street, Columbia Street and Jersey Street. The whole area is an excellent example of successful urban renewal on a human scale.

At the northern end of Fairview, adjoining Prestbury Road, is a development on a rather larger scale. Portland Square was laid out from 1827 onwards by a butcher named Joseph Hughes, who built what is now the 'Sudeley Arms' as his own house. The intention was to create a fashionable residential Square, paralleling the new Pittville Estate on the other side of Prestbury Road. Unfortunately, Hughes went bankrupt, and during the 1830s, his plans were amended and the Square's intended central garden was built over for housing, so that Portland Square is no longer a 'Square' at all. Despite this, a number of fine houses remain, on a grander scale than the rest of Fairview, particularly in the terrace now known as Albert Place, formerly the north side of Portland Square, with good fanlights and two houses with attractive pedimented doorways.

FAITHFULL, LILIAN

To follow Miss **Beale** in 1907 as Principal of **Cheltenham Ladies' College** was not the intention of Lilian Faithfull - until she had attended her memorial service in St Paul's Cathedral as representative of Kings College Women's Department. But so captured was she by the vision of the Ladies' College's virtual founder and creator that she accepted the position and for the next 15 years her contribution to the school, particularly through World War I, was immeasurable.

As visible reminders in the town of her work the Lilian Faithfull Homes must rank high. In **Suffolk Square** the two large buildings on its east side, formerly a residential hotel, were opened in 1951. Indeed it was here that Miss Faithfull herself spent the last few months of her life and where she died in 1952. Her purpose in founding the homes was to provide accommodation with maximum independence yet security of tenure in homely surroundings as well as in congenial company.

There are two other sites where the Faithfull Homes may be found: St Faith's Nursing Home at the junction of Malvern and Western Roads, and the splendid Astell House, with its conspicuous roof cupola and massive chimney stacks, in Overton Park Road. Appropriately the latter, named after Mary Astell who in the 17th century had planned a College for Women, was built in 1912 with money left by Miss Beale, and served as the Ladies' College Staff House until 1968.

FAUCONBERG, LORD

Among the small number of titled men and women who chose to live at

Cheltenham during the 18th century was Lord Fauconberg, one of **George III**'s gentlemen in waiting. Exactly why he chose Cheltenham is not known, and one can only presume that he found the waters particularly beneficial. What is certain, however, is that William **Skillicorne**, the owner of the spa, built Lord Fauconberg a house on Bayshill in 1781, and that it was at that house that King **George III** stayed during his five week visit to the town in 1788.

Bayshill or Fauconberg House, as it was known, became a popular 'sight' for visitors to the town after 1788, and it was occupied by a succession of notable visitors, before being turned into a Private School in the mid 19th century. Eventually it was acquired by the **Baron de Ferrieres**, who demolished it in 1860 in order to build the large red-brick Sidney Lodge, now occupied as a boarding house for the **Cheltenham Ladies' College**.

Given Lord Fauconberg's role in facilitating King George's visit to the town, it is not surprising that he has been commemorated by the name of Fauconberg Road, and by another Fauconberg House, at the corner of Bayshill Road and St George's Road. That house, an imposing villa, also now occupied by the Ladies' College, was built for a prominent local surgeon, Dr Charles Fowler, in 1847; like a number of nearby houses, it was designed by the local architect, Samuel Onley.

FESTIVALS
An important aspect of Cheltenham's civic activity, providing perhaps a successor to the social 'routs' and fashionable entertainments in the annual round, has been its Festivals. There have been two strands: the sporting, represented by **Horse Racing**, or more accurately the National Hunt Festival, and **Cricket** Festival; while the arts have the International Festival of **Music** as it is now called, the Competitive Festival of Music, and the Festival of **Literature**.

FORBES, JOHN
The architect John Forbes, born c.1790, is best known for designing two of Cheltenham's finest Greek Revival buildings: the **Pittville Pump Room** and **St Paul's Church**. He was also responsible for designing the basic layout of the **Pittville** Estate, and perhaps also for some houses at **Montpellier** and in **Imperial Square.**

In addition to his career as an architect, Forbes also dabbled in building speculation during the late 1820s and early 1830s, buying land and building houses on borrowed money. Unfortunately, he got into debt and, in 1834, foolishly forged a bill of exchange with the signature of a developer and business associate named William Prosser, who Forbes later claimed owed him money. When the bill -which he used to settle his debts with a local

The auditorium of the
Everyman Theatre

No 31, Montpellier Villas
home of John Forbes

Electricity sub-station,
Clarence Street

butcher - was discovered to be a forgery, Forbes was arrested, and at his subsequent trial, was sentenced to transportation for life. Fortunately, a petition to have the sentence reduced was successful, and he eventually spent two years in Gloucester Gaol. This seems, however, to have been enough to ruin a promising career. Nothing more is heard of Forbes after about 1838, and the rest of his life is a complete mystery.

GAS WORKS
There has been a gas works since 1823 on the western edge of the town where the **High Street** meets Gloucester Road, but the building which is the most spectacular dates from 1855 to 1875. Standing at the junction of these two roads, it is a rare example of the extravagance such gas works offices could display.

As an expression of the confidence, even arrogance, of Victorian industry it has an affinity with the assertiveness of Cheltenham's **Town Hall,** or **Public Library**.

In style it is an exuberant mixture of Gothic, French and Baronial. The material is bright red brick more akin to Birmingham than here, though the crispness of decoration and excellent jointing lend weight to the tradition that it was built by local apprentices from the Mechanics' Training School.

GEORGE III
Following the advice of his doctors, the King decided to visit Cheltenham for a few weeks in the hope that the spa waters would cure what he called 'a pretty smart bilious attack'. So, leaving Windsor on Saturday 12 July 1788, the Royal Family arrived here late afternoon, taking up their accommodation in Lord **Fauconberg's** Bayshill House. Apart from drinking the water, usually at 6.00 in the morning, there would be a horseback 'airing round the hills' by the King, or he with his family might make visits to such places as Worcester, Cirencester, Tewkesbury and Gloucester. On his Cheltenham days he would walk alone through the town's streets talking to shopkeepers or just any passerby. Dinner was at 16.00, and in the evening there might be another taking of the spa waters. On three occasions the Royal Family visited the theatre, and also attended **St Mary's** church. It is reported that on their first appearance at the parish church, the day after their arrival in Cheltenham, the choir was so unnerved that 'they had not resolution enough to perform', understandable in the circumstances, what with no organ -and the Bishop of Gloucester. However, before the next time 'a very good bassoon' was engaged to accompany the singers, who apparently acquitted themselves to the King's satisfaction.

The habit of going out alone not only endeared the King to townsfolk but also resulted in incidents of mistaken identity, as when he rode with a sheep farmer at Birdlip discussing matters agricultural. The farmer asked George III if he had seen the King and if it was correct that he dressed plainly. 'Aye, as plain as you see me now,' came the royal reply.

On the 16 August the royal party left for Windsor, and 'all Cheltenham was drawn out into the **High Street**, the gentles on one side and the commons on the other, and a band playing God Save The King,' as Fanny Burney described it.

However, though the Visit was over, its effect in including Cheltenham on the fashionable spas circuit was crucial and long lasting.

GLOSTER AIRCRAFT COMPANY

The 'Gloucestershire Aircraft Company', as it was originally known, was established in 1917, following the involvement of its parent Company **H.H.Martyn & Co** in the production of aircraft components from 1915 onwards. Its first Chairman and Managing Director was H.H.Martyn's son, Alfred W. Martyn. The Company's name was changed to the 'Gloster Aircraft Company' in 1926.

All the Company's aeroplanes were manufactured at Martyn's Sunningend works at **Lansdown** until 1925, when a gradual move to Hucclecote, near Gloucester, began. The GAC, which eventually became part of British Aerospace, did much to establish the present important role of Cheltenham and Gloucestershire in the aeronautical industry. Among its early employees was Sir George **Dowty**, who worked for GAC as a draughtsman between 1924 and the establishment of the business that still bears his name, in 1931.

GLOUCESTERSHIRE DAIRY AND CREAMERY

In 1876 Miss Mary Butler, soon to become Mrs Holborrow, started a dairy business in **Clarence Street**. She provided pony traps for the milk rounds, and each day the uniformed staff drove them up the **Promenade** and through **Montpellier**. The traps were painted patriotically in red, white and blue, and were the first trade vehicles allowed to go along the Promenade. Five years later the business moved to 2, now numbered 23, Promenade. Not only was this the shop, offices and bottling centre but soon there appeared above the ground floor an open air roof garden cafe. The ironwork can still be seen.

Around 1928 the stables behind **Alma House** were bought, the residual hay proving useful for the dairy van horses that were accommodated there. Today Imperial Lane is still used by the company. The horses have been replaced by motorised power, the offices and bottling department have taken over, but the same family owns the concern; the present managing director married the granddaughter of Mrs Holborrow's son. Few Cheltenham businesses can boast such continuity.

GODING, JOHN

Born in 1816, John Goding was not the first of Cheltenham's historians, for John Prinn may claim that his account in the closing years of the 17th century made an attempt at providing some record of the town's past. However, since that work has almost entirely been lost, it is to Goding that the distinction of being the author of a pioneering project must be given.

He was a grocer by trade, an Assistant Overseer of the Poor, a member of the parish Vestry and most importantly for later generations a man who represented the ideal amateur historian: keenly interested in the past, eager to learn from the memories of his contemporaries and aware of the value of written records. His *History of Cheltenham* was published in 1853, with an enlarged edition 10 years later. Though it inevitably included some inaccuracies present in earlier guides to the town, the amount of information collected, its range of material and the detailed chronology almost year by year make it fascinating reading and invaluable as reference even today.

Goding lived in Burton Street and then at 3 Portland Street opposite the **Masonic Hall**, where he died in 1863.

GORDON, ADAM LINDSAY

A pupil at **Cheltenham College** where his father was a master, Adam Lindsay Gordon lived during those early years at 28 Priory Street. Preferring the company of boxers and horse trainers, he became friendly with such persons as James Edwards, middle weight champion, whom he once knocked out, Tom Oliver, George Stevens and Tom Pickernall, who as 'Mr Thomas' rode in sixteen Grand Nationals and won three times.

Himself a skilled rider, Gordon wrote the poem *How we beat the Favourite* after the Cheltenham Steeplechase of 1847. However, his father decided the boy should seek his fortune in Australia, and his subsequent life there resulted unexpectedly in the flowering of his poetic talent. Indeed, he was eventually considered that country's national poet. He died in 1870, aged 37.

GOVERNMENT COMMUNICATIONS HEADQUARTERS

GCHQ, the Ministry of Defence's top secret 'listening post', is one of Cheltenham's largest employers, and is one of the things that people immediately think of when Cheltenham is mentioned, because of a spy scandal there in the early 1980s and the banning of its independent Trade Unions 'in the interests of national security' in 1984. The latter ultimately led to the sackings of a number of employees who refused to give up what they considered a basic human right, and to annual protest marches through the town, which still take place, the matter being as yet unresolved.

GCHQ has two bases in Cheltenham, each with striking modern buildings. One is to the north-east of the town, at Oakley, while the other is at Benhall, to the west of the town, along Gloucester Road.

GRAMMAR SCHOOL

Founded in 1578 by **Richard Pate**, the original site in the **High Street** having long since been given over to shops, this school is now located on the western side of the town, in buildings entirely of the modern idiom. Its history is not without interest. In the early years, an entrance charge of 8p was expected from the boys living in the parish, but double that for outsiders. A pupil who was absent for more than 4 days, 'especially at harvest time' had to pay again on re-admittance. The income from this source was spent on books that were to be 'tied with little chains'.

Unfortunately the endowment by Pate was not responsibly administered by the Fellows of his old college at Oxford, and by the early 19th century legal action had to be brought against Corpus Christi College to ensure survival.

Survive it did, though in the process it lost its original and Victorian buildings. What it retains is its list of past pupils. With such names as Frederick **Handley Page**, Gilbert **Jessop**, Benjamin Baker, who constructed the Forth Railway Bridge, and Gustav **Holst** amongst them, Pate's hopes will not have been disappointed. And now the sister establishment, the Grammar School for Girls, opened in 1905, has joined from its site in Albert Road.

GUIDE BOOKS

Because Cheltenham was a popular resort from the 18th century onwards, it was inevitable that a succession of guide books to the town would be produced for its visitors - a process that still continues to this day. The earliest of the guides was published in 1781, and rejoiced in the name of *The Cheltenham Guide: or, useful companion, in a journey of health and pleasure to the Cheltenham Spa*. Like its successors, this first guide contained a wealth of information about the town, which is, of course, as valuable to local historians today as it was to visitors in the past.

A stream of guide books followed in the years after 1781, published by, amongst others, Simeon Moreau, Cheltenham's first **Master of the Ceremonies**, and a number of local librarians. Most of them were illustrated by engravings, lithographs or woodcuts, thereby giving us many fine images of the town. Perhaps the most intriguing of all the guides - and one that has been reprinted twice in recent years - was George **Rowe**'s *Illustrated Cheltenham Guide* of 1845. In a series of four walks, Rowe takes the visitor on a tour of the town, with an emphasis on its modern achievements. Despite the many changes that have taken place in

corner shop in
Fairview

Gasworks
offices

George III

Gloucs Dairy
& Creamery,
Imperial
Lane

Cheltenham since Rowe's day, it is still possible to follow his routes, and to identify many of the buildings that he describes.

GYM CENTRE, MONTPELLIER
The many visitors to **Montpellier Gardens**, whether to play tennis, stroll, or have a work-out at the Gym Centre probably give hardly a second glance to the tiled roof and half timbered end of that building. Yet this was, in the earlier years of this century, the stage and dressing rooms of an open air theatre. The audience sat where the main building has been added, and dual purpose seats with reversible backs were used, so that they could serve for bandstand audiences in the opposite direction. Incidentally, the **bandstand** itself is of interest.

HALL, MARIE
The violinist Marie Hall was born in Newcastle in 1884, and though she did not go to one of the recognised music colleges in this country there were occasional lessons from such illustrious persons as Elgar and Wilhelmj. On the advice of Kubelik she went to Prague, studying with Sevcik. Her debut in Vienna in 1903 signalled the start of a solo career that took her all over the musical world. Her first visit to Cheltenham was in 1905, and she made the town her permanent home in 1911 when, having married Edward Baring, the couple moved to 9 Eldorado Road. In 1984 a plaque was unveiled to commemorate her residence there till her death in 1956, and appropriately it was done by Ursula the widow of Vaughan Williams who composed for, and dedicated to, the violinist his wonderful 'Lark Ascending'. Indeed she gave it the first performance in 1921.

HARRIS, ARTHUR TRAVERS
Son of an Indian Civil Service officer, Harris went out to Rhodesia at 16, joined the army as a bugler and transferred to the Royal Flying Corps in World War I. His role in World War II was better known. For in 1942 he became Air Officer Commanding-in-Chief, Bomber Command. By the time he died in 1984 he had become a Marshal of the RAF, 'Bert' or 'Butch' to countless air crews, and as 'Bomber Harris' a legend to the public. In 1982 he came to Cheltenham to unveil a plaque at 3 Queens Parade where he had been born in 1892.

HIGH STREET
Cheltenham's bustling and much-rebuilt High Street is at the very heart of the town's history, for until the early years of the 19th century, when the Regency town began its great outward expansion, the town consisted of little more than the High Street, plus a few lanes and alleys leading into the

adjoining fields. Indeed, so prominent was the High Street in pre-Regency Cheltenham's topography, that the town itself was sometimes known as 'Cheltenham Street'.

Here, in its High Street, were the houses, shops and inns that made up Cheltenham, many of its buildings dating back several hundred years, and being of timbered construction. Inevitably, the growth of Cheltenham led to a change. The buildings of the High Street were gradually rebuilt or at least refronted, and its appearance began to alter. But its importance did not, and it remained the commercial heart of the town throughout its heyday, including along its length the **Assembly Rooms** and the principal coaching inns, most notably the Plough Hotel.

In more recent times, however, much of this once fine street's architecture has been lost to modern redevelopment. During the 1960s, several of its most historic buildings, including the Victorian **Grammar School** and the Original **Brewery** were swept away for a concrete block between Henrietta Street (formerly Fleece Lane) and North Street (formerly Greyhound Lane), while more recently, the building of the **Regent Arcade** has meant the end of the Plough Hotel.

Even so, the High Street still has much of interest, in addition to excellent shopping, and its changing nature reflects the varied nature of the town itself. In the east, adjoining London Road, the Upper High Street is largely residential, continuing London Road's fine succession of Regency houses. Once past the entrance to Sandford Park, however, the street becomes commercial with a mix of small shops and multiple stores. This theme is continued more or less to St George's Square, where a further change begins to take place. Between there and the Tewkesbury Road is the Lower High Street (or Lower End), older in feeling and smaller in scale, with many small businesses, including several second-hand shops. Here more of the past has remained, many of the buildings having tell-tale high-pitched roofs which suggest timber-framing behind later facades, as is so often revealed when properties are rebuilt. Here too are reminders that this part of High Street was also once fashionable, such as the occasional bow-fronted house, or a restored Georgian fanlight. Off both sides of the Lower High Street run narrow streets of small houses, the oldest part of the town's distinctive **St Paul's** area.

Former HIGHBURY CHAPEL

Now a Youth Club Hall, this attractive pedimented chapel on the west side of Grosvenor Street was built in 1817-18 for the use of the Revd Thomas Snow, a Strict Baptist, who had previously ministered at **North Place Chapel**. It was acquired by the Congregationalists in 1827, and served them until replaced by a large new chapel (now demolished) in Winchcombe

Street in 1852.
Despite its secular use, the chapel retains its attractive cast-iron gallery and is worth looking into if open.

HOLST, GUSTAV

Perhaps Cheltenham's most famous 'music son', Gustav Holst was born in 1874 at what was then known as 4 Pittville Terrace, Clarence Road. Today it is a museum in his memory, bearing a plaque unveiled in 1949 by his lifelong friend, the composer Vaughan Williams. The house had only been lent to the family by Mrs Holst's father, Samuel Lediard a solicitor from Cirencester, so when she died in 1882, a move was made to 1 Vittoria Walk. As a boy Gustav was shortsighted and asthmatic, but his musical powers showed themselves at an early age. When only 4 years old he was taken to **All Saints Church** where his father was organist. On hearing something he was already learning on the piano, he called out, 'that's my tune'. Later he sang in the choir, or played violin and trombone in his father's small orchestra. By 1891 he had composed Four Voluntaries for Organ and had the experience of hearing his Scherzo performed by the orchestra at **Montpellier Spa** Rotunda. Holst was a pupil at the **Grammar School** where his father taught music, and his operetta 'Lansdown Castle' - a tollgate in Gloucester Road - was performed at the Corn Exchange in the **High Street**.

At the age of 17 he was appointed organist and choirmaster of St Laurence, Wyck Rissington, travelling by train to neighbouring Bourton-on-the-Water on the Friday and returning each Monday morning. However after a year he had to relinquish the post, together with that of conductor of Bourton's choral society, when he became a student at the Royal College of Music, London.

His subsequent career belongs to places other than Cheltenham, though when, in 1927, 7 years before his death, the Birmingham Orchestra under the baton of Adrian Boult performed his works at a festival concert in the **Town Hall,** Holst was present despite illness, and indeed managed to conduct 'The Planets' himself. Afterwards he asserted it was 'the most overwhelming event of my life'.

HOLST BIRTHPLACE MUSEUM

The small Regency house in Clarence Road, **Pittville**, where the composer Gustav **Holst** was born on 21 September 1874 is now a museum dedicated to Holst's life and work, with period rooms from the Regency to Edwardian periods.

Displays about Holst himself, including his grand piano, occupy the ground floor, while on the first and second floors are a Regency sitting room and a Victorian bedroom and nursery. 'Below stairs' is a working Victorian kitchen and laundry complete with butler's pantry and housekeeper's room.

The museum is an ideal place to recapture something of the atmosphere of domestic life in Cheltenham during its Regency and Victorian heyday.

HOLY TRINITY CHURCH

The first new church to be built in Cheltenham since medieval times, G.A.**Underwood** was its architect. He supervised its erection in 1820-3 at exactly the same time as he was concerned with the **Masonic Hall**, though each has a very different style. Holy Trinity has a Gothic simplicity, its tower even more so with the removal of its pinnacles. Inside almost all available wall space is given over to memorials to 'India in Cheltenham' - retired civil servants or Army Officers. Just outside the tower is Katherine **Monson**'s grave slab. Like **Christ Church**, it has a north-south alignment.

Holy Trinity was the first of several churches in Cheltenham that were built on the 'proprietary system', whereby the money was raised by the sale of shares, shareholders being entitled to the use of a pew - and non-shareholders having to pay to attend services!

HOOPER'S

One of the most impressive facades in the northern part of the **Promenade** is that of the large shop now known as Hooper's. Built in 1823 it was first occupied by a painter called Millet who, it was said, was 'the only artist successful in discovering the process and vehicle by which Titian and other celebrated masters of the old Venetian school conveyed their colours to the canvas'. Quite a claim!

His house later became better known as the Imperial Hotel, and by 1856 as the Imperial Club, membership being offered to 'resident noblemen and gentlemen' but only after the 'greatest vigilance'. Interestingly and perhaps appositely, it is recorded that at this time neighbouring small apartments were available for what were termed 'fashionable young ladies'.

Within 20 years a more prosaic role followed when the building became the town's main Post Office. By 1904 the balcony, entrance steps and lamp standards had been swept away to permit the addition of the heavyweight porch.

Then in 1987 there was another change of use, to that of a prestigious shop. Extensive restoration took place both inside and out, resulting in a return to 'elegance in the most fashionable and cheerful part of Cheltenham', as an early **guide book** expressed it.

HORSE RACING

Each year thousands, of whom a goodly proportion are Irish, flock to the March meeting at Cheltenham. For many this is the climax of the

Gustav Holst

The Grammar school once in the High St.

Marie Hall

Hoopers

Gym Centre

steeplechase, or National Hunt, season, and its setting represents an experience no other racecourse perhaps can provide. Against a background of the scarp at Cleeve Hill, with the distant Malvern Hills away to the west, the course lies in a hollow, its punishing final uphill furlong being the scene of many thrilling and unexpected finishes.

Racing has itself experienced uncertainties at Cheltenham. In the early years of the town's development as a fashionable resort, meetings were held at Nottingham Hill a few miles away. Then with improved organisation Cleeve Hill was the venue. By 1825 attendances were around 50,000, a large grandstand having been built. However, the contempt and condemnation invoked by the recently arrived parson Francis **Close** had effect, culminating in demonstrations against the sport and in 1830 the burning down of that conspicuous grandstand.

It was then that Lord Ellenborough offered his own land for racing and in 1831 Prestbury Park, the present location was first used. Despite a temporary return to Cleeve Hill when the grandstand was rebuilt, and even shorter uses of Kayte Farm at Southam and Noverton Farm at Prestbury - where incidentally Adam Lindsay **Gordon**'s *How we beat the Favourite* is set - eventually in 1902 racing returned to Prestbury Park.

Development of the course has been spectacular. In 1979 the massive grandstand was opened by HM the Queen Mother, a regular visitor at the National Hunt Festival, and subsequent additions have resulted in the older, Edwardian, buildings disappearing.

Yet such is the magic of the Gold Cup meeting that despite the increasing takeover of glass and steel, Cheltenham racing still has the atmosphere of the days of 'Golden Miller', 'Arkle', and 'Desert Orchid'.

HOSPITALS

The General Hospital in Sandford Road was built in 1848-9 to the design of D.J.Humphris, succeeding the earlier site in the **High Street** at what is now **Normandy House**. Over £2,000 was raised by the townspeople to provide some 90 beds, though perhaps not quite so generous was the patients' diet, being largely potatoes, bread, gruel and beer. Linen was changed but fortnightly, and the regime was somewhat strict, one house surgeon making his patients stand at the foot of their beds military fashion when he conducted his ward round.

St Paul's Hospital was the former workhouse in Swindon Road, its original buildings of 1841 displaying the forbidding character of such institutions. It cost £8,000 and at its opening one description observed that 'no public money has been wasted upon ornament or external decoration'.

Only a little less forbidding is the facade of Delancey Hospital in Charlton Lane, built in 1877 to the design of J.**Middleton**. Here it is not economy Georgian but Gothic style that creates the Victorian institutional atmosphere.

However it must be noted that all three of these hospitals have additions that reflect the contemporary concern for health care. In the case of the General, pastel shades of colour and modern construction are particularly evident in the new extensions in College Road, the pathology department especially.

HOTELS

Like other buildings in the town, hotels have in some cases been adapted from houses, and alternatively have become something else. The Savoy in Bayshill Road began as a private villa, having been built by S.Onley in 1847. Later it served as a boarding house for the **Ladies' College**, before being converted into the Curtis Hotel. Amongst its more recent visitors have been the Beatles and the Rolling Stones. Its conservatory dining room and the fine classical details on its facade are noteworthy.

On the other hand, the Belle Vue Hotel on the London Road, where Lewis Carroll stayed in April 1863, and where the **Cheltenham and Gloucester Building Society** began thirteen years earlier, has ceased to offer accommodation, reverting to private occupation as it was when the Hicks-Beach family had it as a town house.

The Plough, once Cheltenham's foremost hotel before the **Queen's** was built, has now only a reproduction facade in the **High Street**'s **Regent Arcade**, and the Countryside Commission's **John Dower House** has little apart from the porch's Royal Arms to remind us of its past role as the Clarence Hotel. Both the Carlton and the George were converted from houses.

IMPERIAL SPA

The Imperial or Sherborne Spa, though long-since vanished, is worthy of note in that it played such an important part in the life of the town. It was established in 1818 by the developers Thomas Henney and Samuel Harward on what is now the site of the **Queen's Hotel**, and was connected to the town by the Imperial or Sherborne Promenade, a tree-lined drive that was later to become simply the **Promenade**, and the very heart of the town.

The original spa was a small one-storey building, designed by George **Underwood**, and its most striking feature was a large statue of Hygeia, the Greek goddess of health, that stood on its roof. The spa was used for only 19 years, and closed in 1837, when its new owners, the **Jearrad** brothers, decided to replace it with the Queen's Hotel and to concentrate the drinking of the waters on the Montpellier Spa, which they also owned. The building was dismantled and reconstructed further down the **Promenade**, on a site now occupied by **Royscot House**. Sadly, Hygeia does not appear to have survived the journey, as there is no evidence that the statue was replaced in the new position!

For a hundred years, the old spa building served first as a furniture warehouse (called the Imperial Rooms), and then as the **Gloucestershire Dairy**. Finally, in 1938, it was demolished to make way for the **cinema** that preceded Royscot House.

IMPERIAL SQUARE

Like the **Promenade**, to one side of which it is attached, Imperial Square began life as part of the 'walks and rides' of the new **Imperial Spa**. Initially, the centre of the Square was used as a commercial nursery ground, as well as an 'ornamental pleasure ground' for visitors to the spa, and this tradition continues today with the Square's profusion of neatly-planted flowerbeds.

Like the Promenade, too, Imperial Square soon provided ideal building land for the fast-growing town, and during the 1830s, terraces of houses were built on two sides, while on the south - replacing the Imperial Spa - the **Queen's Hotel** was built in 1837-8.

Still large and impressive, the Square must have been even more so before part of its central garden was built on - firstly for the **Winter Gardens** in 1878, and then for the **Town Hall** in 1902-3.

INDUSTRY AND MANUFACTURING

Although never primarily an industrial town, Cheltenham has had a number of noteworthy industrial and manufacturing concerns throughout its history. Like most pre-industrial market towns, 17th and 18th century Cheltenham had its brewers, maltsters, tailors, glovers and shoemakers. It also had, unusually, a short-lived involvement in the cultivation of tobacco, until suppressed by Colonial pressure during the mid 17th century. During the 18th century, the town was renowned for the quality of its white stockings, while its women spun yarn for the Stroud clothiers.

With the advent of the spas, and of polite society in Cheltenham, a number of new luxury-instigated industries developed. Directly related to the spas was the manufacture of Cheltenham salts, which were evaporated from the waters at Henry Thompson's Salts Manufactory in the Bath Road, established in 1810 as part of his new Montpellier Baths, now the **Playhouse Theatre**. Other manufactures that developed during the 19th century were cabinet making, gun making and saddlery (these two no doubt being related, at least in part, to the popularity of the local hunts), watch and clock making and coach building. The latter established a link to the development of transport which later saw Cheltenham as a manufacturing centre for railway carriages, bicycles, caravans and aircraft. The building industry stimulated a number of other concerns, including quarrying on

Imperial Square

Holst's
birthplace museum

Gilbert Jessop

General Hospital

Leckhampton Hill, brickmaking, and the manufacture of ornamental **ironwork.**

This tradition of high-quality work continued into the late 19th century, with the establishment of the town's Art Metalworkers, notably **Marshall's, Letheren's** and **Martyn's,** whose diverse activities included the town's earliest involvement in the manufacture of aircraft, and led ultimately to the establishment of the **Gloster Aircraft Company** and **Dowty's.**

Light industry, engineering and high technology have been the key to Cheltenham's industrial development since the 1930s, and to Dowtys one must add the name of the precision instrument makers, Smiths Industries, as a mainstay of the town's economy.

IRONWORK

It has been asserted that Cheltenham has the finest collection of decorative ironwork on its buildings in the country. Indeed its character has largely been shaped by the combination of delicate balconies and stucco walls. The earliest work was in wrought iron and can be seen on Vittoria House and **Claremont Lodge,** dating from the early years of the 19th century. Simplicity of vertical railings soon gave place to the most popular and ubiquitous 'heart and honeysuckle' design. This combination of a symmetrical pair of heart shapes strengthened with cast iron fan shaped honeysuckle appears on innumerable balconies and verandahs.

Cast iron was used on its own, mainly in heavier, more florid designs, for such additional purposes as porch brackets and shop front crestings. Some good examples too can be found on the bandstand in **Montpellier Gardens,** Royal Parade in Bayshill Road and at **Columbia Place,** Winchcombe Street. Although much of the ironwork is now painted black, there is ample evidence to suggest that it was originally painted green, or even gilded.

The enthusiastic 'salvage drives' during the Second World War deprived Cheltenham of many railings and gates, but where the presence of basements saved the protective ironwork, examples can still be seen of lampholders in **Royal Crescent** and **John Dower House.** A particularly fine pair of gates is at Doric House, St Mark's, the home of one of the ironmakers, W.**Letheren.** Other aspects of ornamental ironwork can be seen with the 'dragon and onion' lampstandards in **St Mary's** churchyard, and the **pillar boxes** dating from Victorian times. As well as Letheren's, two other firms are notable in the production of Cheltenham's ironwork: R.E. and C.**Marshall** and H.H.**Martyn.**

JAY, WILLIAM

Of all the architects who worked in Cheltenham during its heyday as a spa, the one who had perhaps the most unusual career was William Jay (1793-1837), the son of a well-known clergyman, the Revd William Jay of Bath, whose own Cheltenham connections included preaching at the openings of the **Cheltenham Chapel** in 1809 and **Salem Chapel** in 1844.

William Jay lived and worked in Cheltenham from 1824 until his bankruptcy in 1828, and during that time he was responsible for designing a number of very striking houses, including **Columbia Place** in Winchcombe Street, and at least some of the early houses at **Pittville**. Like so many architects of his day, he also acted as a speculative builder, and that is probably what led to his downfall.

What is most interesting, however, is what Jay did before and after his Cheltenham years. Between 1817 and 1824, he was at Savannah in Georgia, where he designed a large number of public buildings and private houses, and is regarded as the city's principal architect of the period. His houses there were amongst the earliest Greek Revival buildings in America, and there are strong architectural affinities to what he later did in England. After his Cheltenham years, Jay's movements are less clear, but it is known that in 1836 he accepted the post of Assistant Chief Architect and Inspector of Works in Mauritius. His time there was, however, short, for he died of cholera barely a year later.

JEARRAD, ROBERT WILLIAM AND CHARLES
Throughout the 1830s, the world of architecture in Cheltenham was dominated by the Jearrad brothers, who designed some of the town's finest buildings, and who guided at least a part of its overall development.

Robert William (1783-1861) was based in Cheltenham and was probably the more influential of the two, his brother Charles (1780-1840) working mainly from London. Their first major involvement in Cheltenham appears to have been the acquisition of Pearson Thompson's interest in the **Montpellier** and **Lansdown** Estates in 1830, which led to the abandonment of **Papworth**'s plans and the introduction of their own designs, including the upper range of Lansdown Place, Lansdown Crescent, Terrace, Parade and Villas - all demonstrating a confident ability to work in a variety of styles, whether Greek, Gothic or Italianate. It was the Jearrads who determined to turn Montpellier into a major shopping area by the development of Montpellier Avenue and Arcade, and it was they who decided to remove the **Imperial Spa** and replace it by the **Queen's Hotel**. Their other two great buildings are **Christ Church** and the now-demolished facade of the short-lived Literary and Philosophical Institution in the **Promenade**, built in 1835.

JENNER, EDWARD
Although it is the town of Berkeley that has most claim on Edward Jenner,

for he was born there in 1749, practised as a country doctor, established his vaccination project in the grounds of his home, and indeed died at the Chantry there in 1823, he did have a period in Cheltenham.

In 1795 he came here, living at first in the Lower High Street before moving to 8 St George's Place. Regrettably this house was demolished a few years ago, but fortunately the building in St George's Road where he gave vaccinations still stands. It was known then as the Pest House; today it is part of the **Spirax Sarco** company.

As well as his pioneering medical work, Jenner's contribution to the town extended to becoming one of 72 Town Commissioners appointed by virtue of the Act of 1806 to oversee the physical well-being of Cheltenham, though it seems his only recorded observation was on the subject of the drains outside his house. Nevertheless he was also a founder of a Literary Society which later became the prestigious but relatively short-lived Literary and Philosophical Institution in the **Promenade**.

However when his wife died in 1815, Jenner decided to return to Berkeley. After all, he had written ten years before to a friend that Cheltenham was too fashionable for him; he preferred his old rustic haunt.

JESSOP, GILBERT LAIRD
Of the famous cricketers who played for Gloucestershire, it is Gilbert Laird Jessop whom Cheltenham has most claim to. Born in the town at Cambray Place on 19 May 1874, his record as a batsman is impressive. Although he did not hit the fastest century he did make six of them within the hour, the one against Yorkshire taking only 40 minutes. Succeeding W.G.Grace as county captain in 1900, he also played for England contributing the invaluable 104 runs in 75 minutes that resulted in a victory by one wicket at the Oval in 1902, after the side had lost 5 wickets for 48.

His nickname of 'The Croucher', his superlative fielding at cover-point as well as his fast bowling earned him a reputation far beyond the town.

JOHN DOWER HOUSE
Now the headquarters of the Countryside Commission, this impressive stone faced building dating from about 1820 was once a boarding house run first by James Fisher and then by Richard Liddell. When in 1827 the Duchess of Clarence stayed here for a few days, Liddell decided to call it the Clarence Hotel. Soon a Royal Coat of Arms appeared on its porch, for the Duchess was to become a Queen as wife of William IV. In 1858 the building was bought by the county authority as a magistrates' office and police barracks, the coat of arms remained, and the Countryside Commission saw no reason to remove it on taking over in 1974. Also preserved is the fine ironwork.

The present name is in recognition of the architect, rambler and enthusiast for access to the countryside who in 1945 had his report outlining the provision of National Parks in England and Wales published by the Ministry of Town and Country Planning. The Dower Report as it came to be known led to an Act setting up these Parks, and the Countryside Commission today has responsibility for advising on their running.

JONES, BRIAN

Brian Jones, who achieved fame as an original member of one of Britain's most successful pop groups, the Rolling Stones, was born in Cheltenham in 1942, and educated in the town. After a short career as a bus conductor and as an assistant on the record counter of a local shop, he went to London in 1961, and, in the following year became an early member of the Rolling Stones, as lead guitarist.

Jones shared in the group's meteoric rise over the following years, but a fast life-style and drugs took their toll of his mental and physical health. In June 1969, after repeated bouts of illness, he left the group, disillusioned with his work. Tragically, he died in a drowning accident the following month. He was buried in Cheltenham Cemetery, in Priors Road, where his grave is still a place of pilgrimage for fans of the group he helped to create.

JONES' SHOE SHOP

Cheltenham's libraries were not always publicly funded, or indeed of a general nature. Back in 1845 **Rowe** in his Guide describes one which stood in the northern part of the **Promenade**. It was known as Wight's Theological Library and contained 'the most interesting and useful works together with a miscellaneous stock of standard literature, prints and stationery'. For, as Rowe put it, 'theology has become so necessary a part of polite education'. Today it is a shoe shop, though its upper floors still keep the appearance that those 19th century seekers after spiritual reading would have recognised, a wrought-iron balcony and ornamental vases on the roof parapet.

JORDAN, DOROTHY

Though born in Ireland and gaining her early stage experience in Dublin, Cork and London, it was her association with the tiny Theatre Royal in Cheltenham's Grosvenor Terrace that led to Dorothy Jordan's success. For she took a leading part in the play *The Sultan* performed before **George III** and his family during those 5 weeks in 1788 they stayed in the town. Not only did she receive their plaudits but the critics decided 'as a comedy actress she has no equal'.

Further, she came to the notice of the future William IV, and in fact became his mistress, bearing him 10 children.

Alpha House, Jenner's surgery

John Dower House

Joseph Pitt House

Jones Shoe Shop

Leckhampton church

Sadly, after 20 years the affair came to an end, and in Cheltenham too. For it was in 1811 while performing at the Theatre Royal, Bath Street, that she received a message from him to the effect that their union must end. She never appeared again on the Cheltenham stage.

JOSEPH PITT HOUSE

In 1842 members of the congregation of **Holy Trinity** church found that their parson, the Revd J.Browne, had been paying the choir himself for the past 14 years, at £65 annually. Not unnaturally they felt this was unfair and decided to recompense and reward this expenditure. A fund was opened, resulting after a short time in over £1,000. Clearly a major gesture was called for, and, unknown to Mr Browne, a house called East Hayes in Pittville Circus Road was purchased and presented to him as a gift!

Later it was used as a Ladies' School or Boarding House, then it became the offices of Walker Crosweller for 15 years. Today SAPA Holdings have it as their headquarters and it has been renamed Joseph Pitt House, after the owner of the Pittville Estate's son who bought this area from Joseph senior in 1830.

KNAPP LANE

Its former name was Workhouse Lane, self explanatory indeed, but the Tudor-like buildings which stand at its end are not the remains of the 1809 project to 'keep the poor judiciously and fully employed' heading pins and mop making. They are in fact the result of the Revd Francis **Close**'s energetic advocacy of providing schools in the town. This one dates from 1856, and for its time it was set out on the grand scale with an accompanying school cottage.

However even this establishment was to have an even grander neighbour in the shape of the St James's Station, making the school almost an island among railway lines.

Now the pupils have long since departed and the place has been converted into a business centre; the trains too have gone but there's one reminder of their era - a curved wall which once marked the existence of a locomotive turntable.

KNIGHT, W.H.

One of the architects working in Cheltenham during the 19th century, Knight was responsible for a number of important buildings in the town. He seems to have been at home equally with the restraint of a classical style, witness his 1837 **Synagogue**, as with High Victorian exuberance in the 1880 Worcester City and County **Bank**, now the Midland; or with the shops in **Montpellier Walk** and the **College Baths**. Perhaps most spectacular is his monumental **Public Library** of 1887 where there is a fine example of his ability to mix classical with romantic feeling.

LANSDOWN

The Lansdown Estate was developed on part of the extensive lands that were purchased from the Revd John Delabere of Southam by Henry Thompson in 1801.

After Henry Thompson's death in 1824, his son, Pearson Thompson, employed the London architect, J.B. **Papworth** to design a fashionable residential estate to adjoin the new road to Gloucester, soon to be known as Lansdown Road. Papworth designed a veritable 'Garden Suburb', with terraces, a crescent and a large square. Work on the houses in Lansdown Place, fronting Lansdown Road, began in 1825, and by 1830 the first 14 houses in Lansdown Place had been completed, as had a pair of semi-detached houses, later forming 1-2 Lansdown Crescent.

Unfortunately, Thompson soon found himself in financial difficulties, and in 1830, he sold out his interest in the estate to R.W. & C.Jearrad, two architects who proceeded to rework Papworth's designs, and to design and develop the immense convex Lansdown Crescent, Lansdown Terrace and Lansdown Parade, all of which date from 1831-48. The Jearrads also designed for the Estate a number of detached and semi-detached villas in the Greek, Gothic and Italianate styles, giving Lansdown a refreshing sense of architectural variety. Among these was the large Gothic Revival house known as The Grange, which was built by public subscription in 1838 for the Revd Francis **Close**. It adjoins **Christ Church**, which was built to serve Lansdown in 1837-40.

The great brick-built, stone-fronted houses of Lansdown epitomise 19th century Cheltenham, with its wealthy leisured class and large households. Late in the century, and into the 20th century, however, the houses proved too big. Many were subdivided, or left uninhabited, and their fabric deteriorated. Only since the 1970s has real progress been made on the renovation of the houses and the revival of the area into one of Cheltenham's showpieces. This renovation work has also included work on the brick-built coach-houses and stables in the lanes at the rear of the great terraces, many of which are now used as offices, studios and garages. It was in one of these former coach-houses, in Lansdown Terrace Lane, that Sir George **Dowty** began the business that still bears his name; the building now has a commemorative plaque.

The name 'Lansdown' was soon applied to an area rather larger than the original estate, particularly that stretching westwards from the 1820s and 1830s developments towards **Christ Church**, Lansdown Railway Station and **St Mark's Church**.

LECKHAMPTON

Lying to the south of Cheltenham, under the brow of Leckhampton Hill, and now part of Cheltenham Borough, Leckhampton still retains in parts its 'village' atmosphere, with a restored but still attractive medieval church and a number of cottages from the 16th century onwards. Its grandest house, however, is Leckhampton Court, now a Sue Ryder home, parts of which are medieval.

Leckhampton's connections with Cheltenham itself are very strong, particularly as at least some of the town's building stone came from the hill. Commercial quarrying on the hill began in the 1790s, with a quarry railway running down to the Malvern Inn, in Leckhampton Road. This was later (1810) extended into Cheltenham, and in 1811 it joined up with the new horse-drawn tramroad between Cheltenham and Gloucester, which gave the quarries access to Gloucester Docks. The quarrying has also given the hill its most distinctive feature, the so-called 'Devil's Chimney', an isolated limestone 'stack', which was almost certainly created by the quarrymen when the now vanished quarry incline railway was cut to one side of it. The Devil's Chimney is clearly visible from parts of Cheltenham, and the hill, which includes the remains of an iron age hill-fort, commands fine overall views of the town.

With the expansion of Cheltenham in the 19th century, that part of Leckhampton parish nearest the town provided ideal building land, and both **The Park** and **South Town** were built in the northern part of the parish. To serve the new inhabitants, a second church for Leckhampton, St Philip's, was opened in 1840, and was replaced, on the same site, in 1879-82 by the imposing church of St Philip and St James, another of **Middleton**'s churches. Like Middleton's other churches, 'Pip and Jim', as the church is familiarly known, was intended to have a lofty spire, but the money was never available, and the present distinctive copper-covered saddleback was added in 1903.

LETHEREN'S IRONWORKS

Although never primarily an industrial town, Cheltenham has a tradition of high-quality manufacturing dating back to the early 19th century, when the town produced such items as coaches, quality furniture and firearms.

This tradition continued into the late 19th and 20th centuries, particularly with the work of a number of leading art metalworkers, of whom the earliest was probably William Letheren (1836-1910), whose Vulcan Iron Works at **Lansdown**, near the Midland Railway Station was established in the 1860s.

Between then and the firm's closure in 1906, Letheren's produced some superb ironwork for clients the world over. Fortunately, many good examples may be seen in Cheltenham, including the chancel screen and font cover of **All Saints Church**, the gates of **Arle** Court and of the **Winston Churchill Memorial Garden** (formerly at Cypher's Nursery Ground in Queen's Road), and the gates of Letheren's own home, Suburban Villa (now Doric House), Church Road, St Marks. Other good examples may be seen in the **Art Gallery and Museum.**

Following the closure of the firm in 1906, its works were taken over by **H.H.Martyn & Co,** a firm which developed still further Cheltenham's reputation for fine craftsmanship. William Letheren's son Thomas joined Martyn's, bringing with him the skills of his father's firm.

LITERATURE FESTIVAL

Britain's first Festival to be entirely devoted to Literature was established in Cheltenham in 1949, and was the brainchild of the Spa Manager, George Wilkinson, in conjunction with the Tewkesbury-based author, John Moore, who served as its first Director.

Each October since 1949 a week or more of lectures, discussions, performances and exhibitions is held within the town, and the Festival is now firmly established as one of the country's principal literary events, most of the great names in modern literature having appeared at the Festival at some time during the past 40 years.

LYPIATT TERRACE

Running southwards from the busy roundabout at Montpellier, where stands the Gordon Lamp, is Lypiatt Road, with one of Cheltenham's latest, and handsomest, terraces. Lypiatt Terrace was built on a piece of land known as 'the Lypiatts' from 1847 onwards, and may have been designed by its principal builder, a man named Richard Keitley. If so, he was a man of great talent, for the terrace is certainly one of the town's best examples of the Italianate style of architecture.

Opposite the terrace and in complete contrast to it, are the large detached houses originally known as Park Place and then as Suffolk Lawn. These were built very much earlier, in the 1820s, as part of James Fisher's Suffolk Estate, and were probably designed by the local architect, Edward Jenkins. Now in use as offices, they are worth careful scrutiny for their attractive architectural details.

McCARTHY, LILLAH

Lillah McCarthy, a leading dramatic actress of the early 20th century, was born on 22 September 1875. The site of her birthplace, adjoining the entrance to the **Regent Arcade**, is marked by a plaque. She was highly regarded for her portrayals of the heroines of Shakespeare and Shaw, and was particularly admired by the latter, who wrote an introduction to her autobiography. In 1905 she married Granville-Barker, director of the Court

Leckhampton Hill

Doric House,
St Marks,
home of
William Letheren

Martins the jewellers shop

Beech House, former home
of Charles Marshall

Theatre, herself subsequently managing the Little Theatre and the Kingsway. Two years after her divorce in 1918, she married Sir Frederick Keeble, an Oxford professor, moved from London to Oxford and soon gave up her acting career. She died in 1960, a quarter of a century after her last stage appearance.

MACREADY, WILLIAM CHARLES

The celebrated Shakespearian actor Macready moved to 6 **Wellington Square** from Sherborne in Dorset. His first wife had died in 1852, and on marriage to his second in 1860 he decided to take up residence in the newly-built terrace of Gothic design in one of Cheltenham's Regency squares. Although 67 years of age and in retirement, he did not put his great abilities to one side, for he continued to lecture and read aloud - a practice developed by Charles Dickens with his books. Indeed, the novelist visited Macready here in Wellington Square. It is worth remembering that the **theatre** in Cheltenham had an illustrious history, and Macready's own stated requirements for an actor advanced the status far beyond the level of earlier practitioners: 'a scholar, an accomplished gentleman with a well-regulated mind and finely cultivated taste'.

MARKETS AND FAIRS

Cheltenham first received the right to hold its weekly Thursday market in 1226, when it was granted a charter by King Henry III, and the market remained the mainstay of its economy until the days of the spas. It also received the right to hold an annual Fair, on three consecutive days in July.

Both the Market and the Fair were originally held in the **High Street**, and gradually permanent market buildings were established. These stood in the centre of the street, more or less opposite the Plough Hotel, the site of which is now occupied by the **Regent Arcade**. The buildings included a Market Hall on stone pillars, reminiscent of those still surviving in other Gloucestershire towns, such as Tetbury and Minchinhampton.

As the town grew and became busier, the presence of the market and its buildings became an increasing problem, and they were cleared away by the newly appointed **Town Commissioners** in 1786. A new Market House was built on the south side of the High Street, west of where **Clarence Street** now joins it, only to be rebuilt in 1808 and removed entirely in 1822 when a new Market House was built to the north of the High Street by Lord Sherborne, Lord of the Manor of Cheltenham. That Market House was reached from the High Street by the new Market Arcade, a row of shops now represented by Benington Street, and originally approached through one of the most unusual structures ever built in Cheltenham, a Moghul Indian style screen. Sadly, it was swept away in 1867, but in its day it was one of the country's most charming examples of the vogue for oriental architecture.

Eventually, even the new Market House proved a problem in terms of access and traffic, and in 1876 a decision was made to remove it altogether to a new site off Gloucester Road, once the site of the Albion Brewery, where Market Street reminds us of its continuing weekly presence.

In addition to this outdoor market, Cheltenham has had covered markets for a number of years. For some years before the building of the Regent Arcade, some buildings at the southern end of the Plough Yard were so used, and, more recently, a covered market has been established in Winchcombe Street, occupying premises that have their own place in Cheltenham's industrial history: the former carriage works of William Miles, who was the town's principal coach and carriage builder during the latter part of the 19th century.

MARTIN'S

One of the oldest businesses to retain its name, the firm of Martin's traces its beginnings back to June 1841 when Samuel Martin moved from his clockmaking and jewellery premises at 401 **High Street** to the Colonnade at the north end of the **Promenade**, thereby acquiring the address of 4 & 5 Imperial Circus.

With his son joining the firm and the addition of a partner from France the shop became known as Martin, Baskett & Martin. Not only was the initial lease of 12 years extended but a branch was opened in Paris. In the 1850s a Royal Appointment was granted as working Goldsmiths, Silversmiths, Watchmakers and Engravers to the Queen.

In 1890 a jeweller from Portsmouth, George Dimmer, bought up the concern but retained the original name. His great grandsons are still directors. Even today French clocks bearing the Martin's title come in for repair, and sometimes they are still addressed to Imperial Circus. The shop has over the years retained much of its original appearance, not only outside where delightful panels and columns in classical style grace the curving facade, but also within where there is an intriguing plaster frieze of cherubs engaged in grape-harvesting.

MARSHALL'S IRONWORKS

Although at least some of Cheltenham's early 19th century ornamental **ironwork** was brought to the town from outside, a significant amount, particularly of wrought iron, was made locally by the firm of R.E. & C.Marshall, which had an extensive foundry near **St James's Square**, by the **River Chelt**.

The firm was established by Sussex-born Richard Eede Marshall, who had settled in Cheltenham by 1822, and took over an ironmonger's shop in the **High Street**. He was a practising ironmaster as well as a retailer, and it is for his elaborate ornamental ironwork, which adorns many of the town's fine buildings, that his firm is best remembered. Particularly good examples are the railings (and possibly the balconies) of the **Municipal Offices**, the railings of Beech Cottage in St James's Square, a superb porch on St John's Cottage, Carlton Street, and the screen of the church of St Philip and St James, **Leckhampton** - the last three examples having elaborate and attractive floral details.

Richard Eede Marshall died in 1850, but the business was continued by his sons, and in fact continued in existence until the 1980s.

MARTYN, H. H. & Co.

The firm of H.H.Martyn & Co. was one of the most important in the industrial life of Cheltenham for more than 50 years, and earned for itself a worldwide reputation for high quality workmanship in wood, stone, metals, plaster and stained glass.

Martyn's was founded by Herbert Henry Martyn (1842-1927), who came to Cheltenham from Worcester in 1866 to work with the sculptor R.L.Boulton. He later formed a partnership with a monumental mason, E.A.Emms, and then, in 1888, set up his own firm, with premises at the corner of **High Street** and College Road. In 1908, he acquired William **Letheren's** Vulcan Iron Works at **Lansdown,** which was renamed Sunningend, a name it retained throughout the firm's existence.

Among Martyns' most notable commissions were the Cenotaph in Whitehall (1919), the Speaker's Chair and Despatch Boxes for the House of Commons (1950) and the pulpit of St Paul's Cathedral (1964). The company also provided the interior fittings of many ocean liners, and of palaces, banks and other public buildings throughout the world. Locally, examples of their work include the reredos in the Church of St Philip and St James, **Leckhampton,** and carvings in **Cheltenham College** chapel, while a number of pieces are displayed in the **Art Gallery and Museum**.

In 1915, Martyn's diversified its activities to include the production of aircraft wings and fuselages, and in 1917 the **Gloster Aircraft Company** was established.

Martyn's continued in existence as an independent company until 1934, when it was taken over by Maples, the London furnishers. Thereafter it traded as part of the Maple-Martyn Group, until it was closed down in 1971. In 1992, however, the name of Martyns was revived once more, by a new firm based at the Sunningend Works.

MASKELYNE, JOHN NEVIL

Born in White Hart Street off the Lower High Street, John Nevil Maskelyne was the son of a saddler but the descendant of an Astronomer Royal. It was whilst working as a watchmaker at 12 Rotunda Terrace, **Montpellier** that he was asked to repair a 'surgical appliance'. He soon realised it was being used by a medium to produce, when attached to the leg, table rappings. So when the American Davenport Brothers came to Cheltenham in March 1865, the 25 year old Maskelyne attended their exhibition of 'Spiritualism' and demonstrated his ability to expose their deceptions. Later that year, with George Cooke, a fellow bandsman and cabinetmaker, he presented his Box Trick at Jessop's Aviary Gardens in **St James's Square**. Thus began a career which took him to London's Egyptian and St George's Halls, and to the heights of success in the world of magic. His famous automata are still prized by such illusionists in the world of magic today as Paul Daniels, who, incidentally unveiled the plaque at Rotunda Terrace. Amongst his other activities Maskelyne invented a typewriter with differential spacing, a coin-operated lock, a ticket punch, and filmed Queen Victoria's Diamond Jubilee.

MASONIC HALL

This is one of Cheltenham's truly monumental buildings, almost intimidating in its eyeless facade to Portland Street. The panels above the niches are the only indication of its function, for they display the masonic symbols.

The architect was G.A.**Underwood** and it is strange that for one who himself was a Mason the design should have included some windows on the north side. They are kept heavily curtained as they are in the core of the building, the Temple, itself containing furnishing reaching back to 1823 when the opening took place. Much of the sumptuous decoration is contemporary, while the organ dates from 1832, thus making it the oldest in Cheltenham.

Freemasonry has always been strong in the town since Foundation Lodge dating from 1753 came here from London via Abingdon. Initially it met in Sheldon's Hotel in the **High Street**, till this present site became available for £600.

Around the Temple walls panels display the names of past officers, and among them are some of Cheltenham's most honoured: **Skillicorne, de Ferrieres**, Henry **Boisragon**.

MASTERS OF THE CEREMONIES

Between 1780 and 1872, the social round in Cheltenham was presided over by a 'Master of the Ceremonies', a position modelled on those in operation in the older spa towns such as Bath and Tunbridge Wells. It was his responsibility to welcome prominent visitors, and to preside over the balls and assemblies at the Assembly Rooms in the **High Street**.

Cheltenham's first M.C. was Simeon Moreau, who also ran one of

H.H. Martyn's works at Sunningend, Lansdown

Spa Pharmacy, No 12 Montpellier Street, formerly Maskelyne's workplace

Milestone in Bath Road

Bath's Assembly Rooms during that city's winter season. His appointment at Cheltenham, by a committee of subscribers to the spa, was not without criticism, and those elements in the town who resented the appointment of an 'outsider' soon lampooned him with doggerel referring to the appearance at the spa of 'an ape in the shape of a beau, by the outlandish name of Simeon Moreau'. Moreau was, however, accepted by all in the end, and he and his successors did good service to the town, creating an ordered social life, based on that of Bath. Of his successors, the longest serving was a man who rejoiced in the name of Col Andrew Hyacinth Kirwan, who held office from 1835 to 1872, and who was one of the great characters in the history of the spa. Sadly for Kirwan, it was his lot to preside over the gradual decline of the spas, and it is indicative of the decline that his resignation, through ill-health, in 1872, was followed by the abolition of the post of M.C., which was no longer deemed necessary.

MIDDLETON, JOHN
Articled to the York architects Pritchett & Watson, John Middleton designed in the late 1840s churches in Darlington and West Hartlepool before coming down, on the invitation of fellow-pupil S.W.Daukes, to Cheltenham. His work in the town was extensive: the churches of **St Mark's** in 1862, **All Saints** 1868, Holy Apostles, **Charlton Kings** 1871, SS Philip & James, **Leckhampton** 1870; he enlarged **Holy Trinity** and **St Luke's**, added significantly to the **Cheltenham Ladies' College** and **Cheltenham College**, and in 1877 was responsible for a complete hospital, the Delancey in Charlton Lane. Add to this a number of substantial houses and the contribution of this architect to the Gothic character of the town is considerable. Admittedly his stature was not that of a Pugin or a Scott, for he tended towards a reliance on the copybook, of which he had many in his library. Indeed it is possible to identify details by reference to them. Nevertheless he could design the dramatic composition, and even if many of his buildings have a certain hardness of surface they are anything but light-weight.

His son, John Henry, was to become curator of the Fitzwilliam Museum at Cambridge, Slade Professor of Fine Art and Director of what was to become the Victoria and Albert Museum in London.

MILESTONE
Not strictly a stone for it is made of cast iron, an interesting survivor from the 1840s can be found in Bath Road on its east side. Triangular in section, on the north or Cheltenham side it states 'To Birdlip 5 miles', on the other face '1 mile to Market House Cheltnm'. This reference is to the 1822 structure provided by Lord Sherborne, situated in the **High Street** where Bennington Street now is. In fact, the corner building there now has above

its shop front a plaque announcing 'Centre Stone'. There is another example of this kind of milestone in the **Art Gallery and Museum.**

MILITARY
Following visits to the spa by notable military men (the **Duke of Wellington** between 1805 and 1828; Sir Thomas Raffles and Admiral Exmouth in 1816; Sir Charles **Napier** in 1848), Cheltenham's mild climate attracted many retired soldiers and colonial administrators after their service overseas. They established the town's 'schools and colonels' image, which lingered until its postwar industrial expansion.

Many of the 19th century's key battles are commemorated in names of streets and houses; and various monuments tell of the town's personal losses. The Peninsular War of 1808-14 named Vittoria Walk; the villa named after the battle of Albuera has been demolished, but a wall sculpture just inside **St Mary's** Church tells of one family's sad pride.

Wellington Mansion and its obelisk survive only as engravings, but are replaced in Wellington Street by a small Waterloo Terrace.

Following the Crimean War of 1854-56, Lord Panmure gave the town a pair of cannons 'taken at Sebastopol'. One ornate plinth has survived, in front of the **Queen's Hotel**, giving names; but the cannons were removed in World War II. The Crimean War's first battle named Alma Road and **Alma House.**

Fanny Duberly retired to **The Park** in 1881. She was the only officer's wife present throughout at the Crimean 'seat of war', and published a Journal, which Queen Victoria found too frank. 'Mrs Jubilee' rode on with the 8th Hussars to the suppression of the Indian Mutiny (1857-59), even joining the cavalry charge at Mongroubee.

General Charles Gordon, who died at the siege of Khartoum, Sudan, in 1884 is commemorated by the Gordon Lamp, near Montpellier Rotunda.

Monuments to the Boer War (1899-1902) are in the **Promenade's** Long Garden and in front of **Cheltenham College.**

MILLS
Of the mills that stood along the course of the **River Chelt**, the most recognisable is that in Vernon Place off the Bath Road. Known in the past as Cheltenham or Cambray Mill, its more familiar name is Barrett's, after a 19th century owner. Over the years its importance to the town in controlling the water supply for cleaning the streets was vital: in 1561 Edward Barthiam was ordered to open the sluice three days each week, and as late as 1813 William Barrett himself had to permit water to flow 'as heretofore' down the **High Street.**

Sandford Mill, though the present structure dates only from the late 18th century, can trace its ancestry to 1086, and its ownership at one time to

Masonic
Hall

Neptune
Fountain

Barrett's
Mill

Municipal
Offices

Cirencester Abbey. The neighbouring field known as Cox's Meadow owes its name to a past miller.

A third mill at **Alstone** can just be identified by stonework at the junction of Great Western Terrace and Millbrook Street.

MONSON, THE HON. KATHERINE

Without doubt, the most unusual person to become involved in the development of the Regency town was Katherine Monson, the daughter of the 4th Baron Monson of Burton in Lincolnshire. Miss Monson was born in 1758, and is believed to have been living in Cheltenham by the 1780s. During the early years of the 19th century, she began buying land to the north of the **High Street**, and between 1805 and 1827, was responsible for building at least 17 houses, including **St Margaret's Terrace**. Despite being over 60 years old by the 1820s, she personally supervised the building work - a rare example of a lady builder, and rarer still given her titled background.

Unfortunately, like so many builders during the second half of the 1820s, she got heavily into debt and was eventually declared bankrupt in 1828, only escaping her creditors by fleeing to France, from where she eventually returned to Cheltenham, to lodge, and eventually to die, in the house of her former clerk of works, William Halford. She was buried in Halford's family grave, which may be seen outside the west door of **Holy Trinity Church**, and is remembered by Monson Avenue, which stands on part of her former property, by the site of Monson Villa, once her home, the site of which is now occupied by the **Brewery** offices.

MONTPELLIER

Cheltenham's 'Continental quarter' as it often known - a reputation based on its distinctive architecture and many cafes and bars as well as on its name - was laid out during the early decades of the 19th century around one of the town's new spas. Like the fashionable areas of several other English towns and cities, including nearby Bristol and Gloucester, it was named after the southern French spa town of Montpellier, a place where many British families were interned during the Napoleonic War.

The founder of Cheltenham's Montpellier was Henry Thompson, who purchased its site from the Revd Delabere of Southam in 1801. He proceeded to build himself a house, which still survives as Vittoria House in Vittoria Walk, and to establish his new **Montpellier Spa**, which was opened in 1809. Tree-lined 'walks and rides' were soon planted in the vicinity of the spa, the **Montpellier Gardens** were laid out , and very soon, villas and terraces to accommodate visitors were built in its vicinity, of which **Claremont Lodge** is perhaps the finest.

Soon after the establishment of the spa, a number of small shops were opened in its vicinity, including an optician's shop and a subscription library, and this set the tone for Montpellier's development as a specialist shopping area, which it retains to this day. Particularly during the 1830s and 1840s, a succession of purpose-built shop were built, particularly those on either side of Montpellier Avenue (including **Montpellier Arcade**) and along the Montpellier Walk, where the trees were cut down and replaced by shops from about 1840 onwards. These are among Cheltenham's most distinctive buildings, each shop being fronted by a **caryatid**. Finally, in 1843, a further block of shops, known as the Montpellier Exchange (now Barclay's Bank) was built to the south of the Spa, on the site of Mawe and Tatlow's Museum, and in 1844-50, more shops were built in Old Well Lane (which was renamed Montpellier Street), on the west side of the Spa, including Rotunda Terrace, part of the **Bayshill Estate**.

Many of these shops catered for the wants of visitors, and luxury items prevailed - glass and china warehouses, high class outfitters and the inevitable chemists and druggists and grocer's shops. Such establishments still predominate today, and a further phase in the area's retail development was achieved in 1985, with the opening of the new **Montpellier Courtyard** development.

MONTPELLIER ARCADE

Cheltenham has one of the best-preserved early 19th century shopping arcades in the provinces - the Montpellier Arcade, built in 1831-2 as part of the **Jearrad** brothers' scheme to create a new shopping area at Montpellier, and barely altered since.

Standing on one side of Montpellier Avenue, the Arcade consisted of 16 shops, half of which were entered from Old Well Lane (now Montpellier Street). It still retains its two entrances, above one of which - facing Montpellier Walk - the incised lettering giving the Arcade's name is clearly seen. The Arcade was described shortly after its opening as 'though not extensive, yet presents a pleasing *coup d'oeil* from the upper entrance. It is furnished with shops and lighted by a glazed roof' - a description that holds true today. Its early businesses were typical of the town's luxury retail outlets - clothiers, chemists, a jeweller, a pastrycook, an artist's repository and a coffee and cigar house.

MONTPELLIER COURTYARD

The most recent addition to Montpellier's speciality shopping area is the £3 million Courtyard development in Montpellier Street, opened in 1985. Twenty-two shops and restaurants, plus some residential accommodation, surround a sunken 'Piazza', with a striking glass and iron pavilion at its centre. The development also involved the continuation of the 1840s Rotunda Terrace, in Montpellier Street, a successful fusion of old and new.

The whole complex was designed by local architects, Ralph Guilor and the Stanley Partnership, in conjunction with Sir Hugh Casson.

MONTPELLIER GARDENS

The Montpellier Gardens were established soon after the opening of the **Montpellier Spa** in 1809, to provide 'an ornamental pleasure ground' for visitors to the spa. Tree-lined drives were created around the edge of the garden, and by 1820 houses were being built on its north and south sides, forming two terraces known originally as North and South Parades, and now as Montpellier Spa Road and Montpellier Terrace respectively.

The gardens themselves were developed over the succeeding years, and combined formal flower-beds with shrubberies and winding paths. Gradually, a number of items of particular interest were added, including a Chinese pagoda, and, from 1834 onwards, the so-called Napoleon Fountain. Always a focus for the social life of the town, the Gardens were a venue for many events, including a number of balloon ascents, which were popular entertainments during the 1830s and 1840s.

With the decline of the spas, the Gardens became rather neglected, but were revived after 1892, when they were purchased by the Borough Council. The lawns and flower-beds were renewed, and new features added, including a **bandstand**, an open air theatre (the remains of which are now incorporated in the **gym centre**), and tennis courts. Once again, the Gardens formed a major amenity in the life of the town, which they continue to do to this day.

MONTPELLIER SPA

In 1809 Henry Thompson, having bought land at Montpellier from the de la Bere family, constructed a wooden pavilion with a colonnade facing the road, to accommodate visitors to his spa. By 1817 it became so popular that he had it rebuilt in stone to the design of G.A.**Underwood** complete with the crouching lion on its parapet. However, Thompson's son Pearson, having taken over the enterprise, asked J.B.**Papworth** to add a dome, in 1826. The result was the magnificent structure seen today. It has similarities to Rome's Pantheon, indeed the dimensions are almost identical: 56ft high, 54ft across. Originally there was a large chandelier and wall mirrors to illuminate the panelled decoration on its interior.

The building became a bank in 1882 when the Worcester City and County Bank occupied one corner, though balls and concerts continued to be held in the main area. For 'taking the waters' had never been a solitary affair, and from 6.00 in the morning till late in the evening visitors would have thronged the spa, paying for its facilities. In 1834 for example, the subscription ranged from 5 pence for a stranger for a morning to £2.10 for a family for the season. Here too was a reading room at one corner and a billiard room at the other, with the boiling house in between.

In 1848 Jenny Lind, the 'Swedish Nightingale', sang in the Spa; in 1891 young Gustav **Holst** heard the first performanance of his Scherzo and Intermezzo here. But it was the use as a ballroom which showed off the glittering events attended by virtually every distinguished personage from the **Duke of Wellington** to the innumerable 'lovely, titled and fashionable'.

MOZLEY, REVEREND THOMAS
The High Church tradition is represented in Cheltenham by the Revd Thomas Mozley who for the last 13 years of his life lived in the town, dying at 7 Lansdown Terrace in Malvern Road, where earlier Sir Ralph **Darling** had his home. However, Mozley had been a resident, albeit for only 5 months, many years before when on leaving Oriel College Oxford with only a pass degree he became tutor in 1828, at the age of 22, to Lord Doneraile's son. His subsequent career in the Church took him to parishes in Essex, Oxfordshire, Northants and Wilts; it also brought him into closer contact with Henry Newman when he married the Tractarian's sister, and inevitably Mozley himself became a leader of the Oxford Movement. When he died in 1893 it was said of him: 'an acute thinker in a desultory sort of way, a man of vast information and versatility and a very delightful writer'.

MUNICIPAL OFFICES
The superb terrace on the west side of the **Promenade** that now includes the Municipal Offices was built in 1823-5, and was originally known as 'Harward's Buildings' after Samuel Harward, one of the developers of the Imperial Estate. Unfortunately, its architect is uncertain, but George **Underwood**, who designed the Imperial Spa, and who may have been responsible for the whole concept of the Promenade, is the most likely candidate.
   The houses were built as private residences, and were described in a local guide book shortly after their completion as 'built after the fashion of the Louvre....if inferior to its prototype in size and grandeur, is yet possessed of local advantages superior in many respects to its more celebrated Parisian model' - though what those advantages were the book fails to tell its readers!
   The houses remained as private residences into the present century, when they gradually changed to commercial or office use. The central houses were gradually acquired, from 1914 onwards, as the Municipal Offices, but although much changed internally, their exterior aspect has been unaltered, and the terrace forms one of the town's finest features. The central portico is especially fine, as is its profusion of ironwork, by

*Scenes
in
Montpellier*

Marshalls of Cheltenham. In front of the terrace are formal gardens - once known as the Long Garden - including a statue of one of the town's most famous sons, the Antarctic explorer, Edward **Wilson**, and Cheltenham's two war memorials, both by Boultons, commemorating the dead of the Boer War and the two World Wars.

MUSIC FESTIVAL
It is fortunate that the county should share in the oldest Music Festival in England, namely the Three Choirs and also have in Cheltenham the oldest of the post World War II music festivals. Indeed the latter was planned in 1944 by George Wilkinson, the borough's Spa Manager, who proposed that at least one new composition by a British musician be included in each programme. Hence when the first event took place a mere 5 weeks after the end of the War in 1945 it was as the Festival of British Contemporary Music. In that year Benjamin Britten conducted the first concert performance of the Sea Interludes from *Peter Grimes*, with William Walton and Arthur Bliss also conducting their own works.

So flourishing has been the growth of the Festival, and so prestigious its programmes that to list all the composers and performers who have been represented or appeared here would read like the index of a book of music. However, the outstanding names must be mentioned if only to convey something of the range: Gerald Finzi, Kenneth Leighton, Malcolm Arnold, Lennox Berkeley, Edmund Rubbra, Elisabeth Lutyens, Matyas Seiber, and of course Vaughan Williams and Gustav **Holst**. For performers the task is impossible, since virtually every 'great name' has appeared on the stage of the **Town Hall** or at the **Pittville Pump Room**.

Since 1974 its title of Cheltenham International Festival has reflected expansion musically by its inclusion of Classical and Romantic works, chronologically in having compositions from all centuries, and geographically in welcoming composers and performers from all countries.

Interestingly too its venues have increased to include not only such places in Cheltenham as the **Everyman Theatre**, but also further afield like Gloucester Cathedral, Tewkesbury Abbey and Berkeley Castle.

NAPIER, SIR CHARLES
It was only after he thought his principal military career was over that Lt-General Sir Charles Napier came in 1848 to Cheltenham. Living at 1 Wolseley Terrace just behind **Imperial Square**, he seems to have made himself very much part of the town, not only by his riding around on an Arab horse, but also in his socialising with the many officers and officials who had served with him in India. Most notable was of course Lord Ellenborough, his Governor-General who had purchased Southam de la Bere just north of the town.Napier's stay in Cheltenham was not destined to

last very long, for with renewed war in the Punjab, he returned there on the insistence of the **Duke of Wellington**'s 'If you don't go, I must'. So a farewell dinner took place at the **Queen's Hotel** on 5 October 1848 attended by Ellenborough, together with some 90 fellow officers, before he received a grand send-off from Cheltenham at the Great Western Railway Station. Perhaps today what is chiefly remembered of Napier is his terse telegraph on recapturing Scinde, 'Peccavi', though the Queen's Hotel does have a bar named after him.

Incidentally, many years later, from 1906 to 1915, the parents of P.G.Wodehouse lived at 3 Wolseley Terrace. What the humorist made of the historical association is not evident.

NEPTUNE FOUNTAIN
A prominent feature of the **Promenade** is the large Portland stone Neptune Fountain, which was constructed in 1893 by the local sculptor, R.L.Boulton, and depicts Neptune being drawn by sea horses. The fountain, which utilises the waters of the **River Chelt** running beneath it, was designed by Joseph Hall, the Borough Engineer, who is said to have been influenced in his choice of design by the Trevi Fountain in Rome. It was unveiled, according to a local newspaper, 'with slight but sufficient ceremony' by the Mayoress on 3 October 1893.

NEWSPAPERS
The 19th century was the age of newspapers, and particularly for Cheltenham with its ever changing society coming to the Spa. Topical accounts of fashionable gossip mixed with increasing political awareness were the ingredients.

In 1883 the *Gloucestershire Echo* appeared on Cheltenham's streets on 9 January, calling itself the oldest in the county, an unusual claim for a new newspaper. Furthermore the *Echo* of 1 January 1873 was numbered 1,469! The explanation lies in the change of name: *Cheltenham Evening Telegram* becoming *Echo*. Publication in those years was from 3 Promenade Place, but in 1891, Promenade House, the former premises of Mr Hale's Piano, Harp and Music Rooms, became its home. Today the newspaper's offices are still there though the printing presses have gone elsewhere.

An even older paper, the *Chronicle*, first published in 1809, began its life in the **High Street** at a building which stands on the corner of St George's Place. When Henry James Cochrane who had been running the paper for many years bought the *Echo* in 1884 the two names were retained. After a year he sold to J.W.Shenton who lasted only 5 weeks before H.Wilkins tried his hand at running the publication. However he had no greater success, and by 1886 the Cheltenham Conservative Press acquired it. In 1894 the business was sold for £700, but 18 years later it fetched

Normandy House

Oriel Lodge

Promenade House, home of the 'Gloucestershire Echo' since 1891

£17,500.

Many other newspapers flourished according to their political allegiances. At 19 Clarence Street the *Examiner* was the Liberals' mouthpiece and the building provided in October 1862 a strange phenomenon. Apparently a suspended letter file began swinging continuously till the following February, despite attempts to steady it. Reports assert that even scientific investigation failed to find an explanation. However as it proved quite an attraction maybe the publicity was not unwelcome!

The Radicals' paper the *Free Press* lasted from 1834 to 1908, and the Conservatives' *Journal* from 1824 to 1868, but for the local historian the *Looker-On* provides invaluable information about Cheltenham social activities and personalities for the period 1834 to 1920.

NORMANHURST

It stands in Christchurch Road looking more like a French chateau than a Victorian town house. The stonework is a riot of carving: lions' heads, sun rays, birds of all descriptions, even a Jack-in-the-Green. Strange therefore that the house should have been built by a family with the very ordinary name of Smith. That was in 1882. A later resident was somewhat more colourful. Stella Louise Ingram lived here from 1933 to 1979, and those who remember her may have known her as a formidable magistrate in the town.

Interestingly, six of the houses along neighbouring Queen's Road have similar carving around their front doors. Each one is differently treated: one has elaborate vases, another dolphins. There is a boy stealing eggs from a nest, and again heads, a squirrel and popinjays can be found as at Normanhurst.

NORMANDY HOUSE

This building at the spot in the **High Street** where Ambrose Street branches off has seen not only great changes but also experienced them itself. Built as a private house, its name Segrave House showed association with the **Berkeley** family. By 1839 an additional block was needed, for the place had now become the town's General Hospital, and space was required for two 20-bed wards as well as an operating theatre. So the building assumed its lop-sided appearance in the interests of health. Education followed, for 10 years later it became the St Mary's Hall for women students of the Teachers' Training College in Swindon Road. Then after another 20 years the name and role changed again. As Idmiston House it served as offices for the Inland Revenue and the Department of Social Security. Finally, it is today called Normandy House and meets the needs not of health, education or taxation but of the holidaymaker who wishes to go to France.

NORTH PLACE CHAPEL

Perhaps the most attractive of all the town's Nonconformist chapels, North Place Chapel was built in 1816, as a private chapel, by a wealthy local magistrate, Robert Capper, who lived at the now-demolished Marle Hill House, the grounds of which now form the western extension of **Pittville Park**.

The chapel, which was also known as Portland Chapel, is of brick cased in ashlar stone, and was probably the first Gothic Revival building to have been erected in Cheltenham; its Greek Doric portico was not added until 1865, and may have come from another local chapel.

In 1819, the chapel was gifted to the Countess of Huntingdon's connection, which owned it until recent years, when it was acquired by a congregation that formerly met in a chapel in the Golden Valley, towards Gloucester. Although extensively restored in recent years, its future use is unfortunately now uncertain.

ORIEL LODGE

In a town so thoroughly classical in its buildings it comes as a relief to find examples of Gothic. One such is Oriel Lodge in Oriel Road. Designed by Edward Jenkins, who was also responsible for the church of St James in **Suffolk Square**, it was built in 1823 for Charles Timins, a retired sea captain in the East India Company. There is a story that the front garden, now merely asphalt car parking, once boasted a willow tree grown from a cutting that Timins had brought back from the tree that grew beside Napoleon's temporary grave in St Helena. Indeed it seems he also distributed other cuttings which were planted at the **Neptune Fountain** in the **Promenade** and in gardens on Lansdown Road.

One of Oriel Lodge's later occupiers was Miss Graham-Clarke, reputedly the favourite aunt of Elizabeth Barrett Browning. However, the Timins family's association persisted as late as 1931 when Mrs W J Haslam the great grand-daughter of Charles sold the house to the General Accident Insurance Company. Since then it has been head-quarters for the Polytechnics Clearing House, and offices for **Eagle Star**.

PAGE, FREDERICK HANDLEY

The son of a Cheltenham upholsterer, Frederick Handley Page was born in 1885 at 3 Kings Road, a semi-detached 19th century villa standing in a quiet suburban area of the town. After attending the **Grammar School** and Finsbury Technical College, he set up in 1909 a company to build aircraft. His first monoplane flew in the following year, and in 1911 he produced the first passenger-carrying monoplane to cross London. But the company made its reputation in World War I with the Royal Naval Air Service twin-engined bomber, and a four-engined version that was able to attack Berlin. Both of these aircraft became the first planes to fly from England to India. In World War II such types as the Hampden and Halifax represented his company's products, but many aviation historians will assert that the most beautiful and reliable civil aircraft ever produced was the HP42 'Heracles' class used by Imperial Airways between the Wars. Sir Frederick died in 1962.

PAPWORTH, JOHN BUONAROTTI
In terms of national reputation, John Papworth (1775-1847) was the most important architect to work in Cheltenham during the early part of the 19th century, although the number of buildings that may be attributed to him is rather limited, as several of his commissions eventually came to nothing.

Papworth's office was in London, and exactly how he came to be involved in Cheltenham is a mystery. His first commission, however, appears to have been the design of a house called Rosehill, to the north of **Pittville**. The house was built in 1824-5, for a Bath doctor, John Shoolbred, who had decided to move to Cheltenham.

Between 1825 and 1829, Papworth's principal client in Cheltenham was Pearson Thompson, for whom he designed a drainage system for the **Montpellier Gardens**, a scheme for the development of the **Lansdown** Estate, including plans and elevation for houses in Lansdown Place and Lansdown Crescent, and various alterations to the **Montpellier Spa**, including the fine dome or Rotunda, which distinguishes the building today. Other important commissions included the reworking of Edward Jenkins' designs for **St James's** Church and the designing of the now-demolished St John's Church in Berkeley Street.

However, it is Papworth's design for the Cheltenham 'standard villa' that is most recognisable around the town: a facade having a classical porch flanked by windows beneath recessed arches. The building now called Regent House at the corner of Vittoria Walk may be considered the prototype, dating from 1825.

PARAGON PARADE
Although now known simply as 114 to 136 Bath Road, this terrace was once called Paragon Buildings or Parade. Here the novelist Anthony Trollope lived for a year, during his career with the Post Office. At 118, Duncan Gordon Boyes had his home before joining the Royal Navy. In 1864 as a midshipman he was awarded the Victoria Cross for carrying the Queen's Colour under intense fire. Tragically he was court martialled later for a comparatively minor offence, and at the age of 23 committed suicide.

Incidentally the gate piers have early 19th century iron lamp holders possibly dating back to the years before gas lighting had come to that part of town.

PARKS AND GARDENS
Cheltenham's reputation as 'The Garden Town of England' depends very much on its 600 acres of parks, gardens and open spaces, and on the year-round floral displays that won for the town the coveted 'Beautiful Britain in Bloom' trophy in 1985 and 1988. Throughout the spring and summer, Cheltenham is ablaze with colour - not only in its public parks, but also in many private gardens, while a profusion of hanging baskets on houses, pubs, shops and offices adds a further dimension to the town's floral quality.

Amongst the town's historic gardens are those at **Pittville, Montpellier** and **Imperial Square**, each of which was created as 'pleasure grounds' attached to the spas. During the past century, a succession of new parks and Recreation Grounds has been provided by the Borough Council, most notably the 14 acre Sandford Park, on the east side of the town centre, opened in 1927, to which Cheltenham's open air swimming pool was added in 1935. Other important suburban parks include Hatherley Park, and the Agg-Gardner Recreation Ground to the west of **Pittville**.

PARK, THE
When Thomas Billings, a solicitor, bought the pear-shaped area of land in **Leckhampton** parish to the south of the town in 1831, he had ambitious plans for its development. Within two years he had started laying out what was intended to become the Gloucestershire Zoological, Botanical and Horticultural Gardens. There would be such exhibits as monkeys, polar bears, kangaroos, pelicans and Golden Eagles, as well as a labyrinth, water cascade, hermitage and curator's house. However, despite the high hopes, the issue of 4,000 shares at £5, and indeed an official opening on Queen Victoria's Coronation Day, 28 June 1838, the enterprise failed. The property was sold soon after to S.W.**Daukes** who converted it into public pleasure grounds, retaining the lake and the broad avenue still known as the Elephant Walk. It is recorded that of the 20 acres, fourteen were retained as promenades and lawns while the remainder were set apart for cricket, archery and other sports. Admission was one shilling (5p).

Around the Park substantial villas were built, Daukes himself designing a (now-demolished) Gothic mansion called Tudor Lodge for his own use. Perhaps the most dramatic that the architect produced was the Italian style lodge at the entrance known now as Cornerways, though in 1855 it was called the Park Spa.

Since 1931 this fine example of 'rus in urbe' has been in the possession of a college, first St Mary's Training College for Teachers, and now the

Regent House, designed by Papworth

The Park

Playhouse Theatre

Pillar box in Bayshill Road

Cheltenham and Gloucester College of Higher Education. Of its many trees mention must be made: there are fine specimens of Wellingtonia, Monterey Cypress, Deodar, Glaucus Atlas Cedar, Tree of Heaven, Austrian and Bhutan Pine.

PATE, RICHARD

Born in 1516, Richard Pate is chiefly remembered by the **Grammar School** and the **Almshouses** he founded. His early years are somewhat obscure, but it is probable that he attended the school run by the parish church. Subsequently he went to Corpus Christi College, Oxford, then in 1541 to Lincoln's Inn. Becoming a barrister, he purchased property which in 1586 he made over to his old college for the purpose of endowing the school and almshouses.

He was Member of Parliament for Gloucester as well as its Recorder, building Matson House just outside that city in 1575. He died in 1588, and his memorial can be seen in Gloucester Cathedral.

PHILLIPPS, THOMAS

Perhaps the world's greatest collector of manuscripts, Sir Thomas Phillipps was born in Manchester in 1792. Whilst at Rugby School his obsession began, spending all his pocket money on everything that lay within his reach, as he wrote, 'whether good or bad, particularly those on vellum'. He became in fact a 'vello-maniac' seeking to preserve whatever he could find, hoping to save them from destruction by deliberately forcing up the price.

From 1820 he roamed Europe in search of manuscripts for five years, and on returning still kept in touch with the leading continental dealers.

In 1863 he moved his massive library from Broadway to its new home in the recently-purchased Thirlestaine House, now part of **Cheltenham College**. Unsurprisingly it took 103 wagons drawn by 230 horses in the charge of 160 men, and many were the mishaps of broken wheels or axles before the whole operation was finished.

Phillipps also maintained a private press so that he could print catalogues of his holdings. When he died in 1872 the collection amounted to over 60,000 manuscripts together with 100,000 books. Sadly this great treasure did not remain intact or pass into one of the national libraries, but was dispersed at sales between 1889 and 1908. Perhaps his example remained to inspire such persons as Ronald **Summerfield**.

PITT, JOSEPH

Joseph Pitt, the developer of **Pittville**, Cheltenham's largest early 19th century building estate, was the epitome of the self-made man of the Georgian era.

Born to yeoman parents at Little Witcombe, near Cheltenham, in 1759, he entered a Cirencester solicitor's office at an early age, and became a lawyer in his own right in 1780. He invested the profits of his legal business in banking, brewing and the purchase of land in Gloucestershire and Wiltshire, acquiring a 'country seat', Eastcourt House, near Malmesbury. Between 1812 and 1831, he served as MP for Cricklade, where he owned half the town's houses.

Pitt began to purchase land in Cheltenham in 1800, including Church Meadow, where the **Royal Crescent** was built, and 'The Marsh', to the north of the town, where **Pittville, Pittville Circus** and part of **St Pauls** were later built.

Unfortunately, Pitt eventually overstretched his financial resources. The only partial success of Pittville, and other business difficulties, led him to borrow heavily from 1824 onwards, and at the time of his death in 1842, he was in debt to the tune of over £50,000, his entire estate being sold for the benefit of his creditors in the following years.

PITTVILLE

The largest and most ambitious of Cheltenham's new building estates of the early 19th century was the brainchild of Joseph **Pitt**, who acquired much of its future site at the time of the 'inclosure' of the Open Fields in 1806, and added further land by purchase during the following years. By the early 1820s, when the demand for land and houses in Cheltenham was at its height, Pitt felt that the time was right to launch his his new 100 acre estate, which he hoped would form a new town, with its own Pump Room, walks, rides and gardens, and building lots for up to 600 houses.

Sadly, despite high hopes, Pittville was never the new town that Pitt had hoped. The building boom of 1822-5 was already past its peak in the spring of 1824 when the new estate was launched, and was to give way to crisis and slump after December 1825. Of the 600 houses that Pitt had hoped would have been built by 1830, no more than 20 had been completed by that year! Despite a revival of building after 1830, barely a third of the intended number were in place by 1860, and even today the total number of houses is not much more than that. Among the developments that never happened were a series of villas between the **Pump Room** and Lake, a great Crescent in the east of the estate, and a church to north of the Pump Room.

That the estate was only a partial success - and, indeed, that it eventually ruined Joseph Pitt - is something of a tragedy, for what was completed is of the highest quality, in terms of both planning and architecture, and Pittville remains one of England's finest examples of a 'Regency' building estate. Indeed, in 1833 one visitor, the Scottish writer Catherine Sinclair, described it as a 'scene of gorgeous magnificence', and drew her readers' attention to the variety of its houses, which were, she remarked, 'of every size, shape and character - Grecian temples, Italian villas, and citizens' boxes, so fresh and clean you would imagine they were all blown out at once like soap bubbles'. The same may be said of Pittville today, and the visitor should look out for the variety of styles and architectural motifs around the estate.

Architecturally, Pittville's high spots are the Pump Room itself, and the villas and terraces of **Clarence Square, Wellington Square** and **Pittville Lawn**, although other attractive houses may be seen in the estate's two main roads - Evesham Road and Prestbury Road. The latter also includes the only shops that were allowed on the estate, including Leamington House, which has been a pharmacy for over 140 years.

As well as the houses, the gardens themselves are worthy of note. The estate includes an artificial lake, created by damming a stream known as Wyman's Brook, which is crossed at each end by an attractive stone bridge of about 1827; that on the west commands a fine view of the Cotswold Hills. To the south of the lake are the lawns of the Long Garden, attractive in themselves and a superb foil to the stuccoed villas and terraces that face them. Halfway down is a refreshment kiosk of 1903 with unusual terracotta dragons on its roof, replacing a small spa well known as Essex Lodge. Like most of Cheltenham's historic parks and gardens, those at Pittville were originally enclosed by railings, and private to the residents and subscribers to the spa.

PITTVILLE CIRCUS

Originally called Albert Circus, after the Prince Consort, Pittville Circus lies on the eastern boundary of the Pittville Estate, and was laid out in 1839-40 by a local builder named Edward Cope, on land purchased from Joseph **Pitt**. The Circus forms an important focus for this part of Cheltenham: through it runs Prestbury Road (an ancient turnpike road), with some of the **Pittville** Estate's attractive houses on its west side. Among these, the villa recently occupied as Christie College seems to match the unusual towered Apsley House, on the other side of the Circus, which was built by Cope in the same year, 1840. To the east of the Circus runs Pittville Circus Road, leading to the All Saints area with many substantial Victorian villas and terraces.

PITTVILLE LAWN

From the entrance to the Pittville Estate, at the top of Winchcombe Street (a spot represented by the fine Pittville Gates, the lower parts of which date back to the 1830s), to the Pittville Lake, the roadway known as Pittville Lawn presents a continuous array of fine houses built between 1832 and 1842. It also exhibits more clearly than any other part of Pittville the architect John **Forbes**'s original intention to provide an architectural rhythm of alternating villas and terraces, particularly in that part of the roadway that faces the Long Garden.

With such an array of houses, it is difficult to single out any for particular mention. However, the three terraces facing the Long Garden (the southernmost of 1826-7 and the other two of 1836-8) are especially fine, with their large Ionic columns and matching ironwork. Of the villas, perhaps the grandest is Dorset Villa of 1840-2, towards the northern end of the Lawn, one of the most extravagant and striking Greek Revival houses of its day. For part of the 19th century, this was the home of the Whinyates, one of the town's leading military families. Most of the other villas are in a similar, if more restrained Classical idiom, though one, Malden Court, built in 1838, is totally different, being in the Gothic Revival style. Its style was no doubt chosen by its builder, a local J.P. named Stubbs Wightwick, for part of the attraction to wealthy intending residents was the fact that the Estate allowed them to build villas in whatever style they wished, unlike the houses in the terraces which were, of course, strictly controlled, even on occasion down to the style of ironwork to be used on them.

PITTVILLE PUMP ROOM
Cheltenham's finest Regency building stands at the north end of Pittville Park, and was built in 1825-30, both as a spa and as the social focus of Joseph **Pitt**'s extensive new **Pittville** Estate. Its architect was a local man, John **Forbes**.

Larger and grander than any of the other spas, the building is two-storied. On the ground floor is a large ballroom, where visitors could meet and listen to a band of musicians, or attend balls, public breakfasts and gala fetes, events that inevitably spilt over into the adjoining gardens. At the rear of the ballroom was the oval pump room itself, where the spa waters were - and still are - available from a marbled pump and counter. Also on the ground floor was a small card room, now converted into a foyer. On the first floor, where the balcony provides a superb view of the interior, and particularly of the dome, the former Reading Room, Library and Billiard Room have been converted into the **Pittville Pump Room Museum.**

Despite the scale and grandeur of its architecture and the initial optimism of all concerned, the Pump Room never lived up to expectations in terms of its success. Already by the 1830s, Cheltenham's spas were competing for a gradually shrinking market, while the successful development of **Montpellier** and the **Promenade** ensured that Cheltenham's fashionable focus remained firmly to the south of the **High Street**, leaving Pittville relatively isolated on the north. Despite the attempts of a succession of lessees to bolster up its fortunes by staging events, exhibitions and flower shows, the Pump Room increasingly became a 'white elephant'.

Eventually, in 1889, the Borough Council bought the building from the County of Gloucester Bank, which had acquired it as part of Joseph Pitt's

Pittville Lawn

Pittville
Pump
Room

Joseph
Pitt

Pittville
Lake

debt-ridden estate, but it was not until after the Second World War that any viable new use was found for the building. Until then, it continued to dispense the waters to a declining attendance, while a major use for the ballroom was as a badminton hall!

Already, by the late 1930s, the poor structural state of the building was recognised, and remedial work begun - only to be interrupted by the war, during which the building was requisitioned as a storage depot by the American Army, while its structure deteriorated still further. In 1949, however, the work of restoration began in earnest, and in 1960, the building was reopened by the 7th **Duke of Wellington**, whose ancestor, the 1st Duke, had watched the progress of its construction 128 years earlier. Now, as well as housing the Pump Room Museum, the building once again provides a major social focus for Cheltenham, particularly with concerts and recitals during the town's prestigious **Festivals** of Music and Literature.

PITTVILLE PUMP ROOM MUSEUM
On the upper floor of the Pittville Pump Room is a museum devoted to the history of costume and fashion from the 18th century to the present day. Each of its twelve display cases contains between one and three costumed figures, and has a painted backdrop showing a scene from Cheltenham's history. The museum also has displays of historic jewellery, and on the history of Cheltenham and Pittville, plus special exhibitions on a costume and textiles theme.

PILLAR BOXES
Cheltenham has some claim to the epithet of 'a pioneer of pillar boxes', for although they were introduced into the Channel Islands in 1852, on the suggestion of Anthony Trollope, writer and Post Office surveyor, there was considerable correspondance between a Revd W.J.Charlton who lived at Lansdown Terrace and the GPO on the usefulness of this item of street furniture.

Reputedly, some of them were put up in the town in August 1854 as an experiment, though this would predate London's, and might be a confusion with the eight which were installed in August 1855. Unfortunately none has survived, but Cheltenham is the proud possessor of eight out of only 94 in the whole country of the hexagonal Penfold type. Made of cast iron by the Cochrane Grove Company of Dudley, they have the royal monogram and coat of arms under decorative tops surmounted by a flower finial. The best examples can be seen in Bayshill, College Lawn, Montpellier Walk and Douro Road.

There are also other Victorian pillar boxes: in Pittville Street, Evesham Road, Lansdown Road, Albert Road and Shurdington Road, while in Great Norwood Street there is one large 'victorian anonymous' box with no initials or coat of arms. Inside Lansdown railway station there survives an Edward VII example, with George V represented by a massive oval double box in the **Promenade**.

PLAYHOUSE

The buildings in Bath Road which today provide the focus for amateur productions opened in 1806 as Henry Thompson's Montpellier Baths. Some 14 warm baths, and one large cold, together with steam rooms enabled ladies and gentlemen 'never being disappointed of a bath even at a minute's notice'. As for the costs: a cold fresh water bath 8p; vapour bath 25p; sulphur bath 15p. Adjoining was Mr Thompson's Salts Manufactory enabling the visitor, having undergone the water treatment, to purchase some of the salts crystalised.

Then in 1898 the Borough bought the place and converted it into a swimming pool. However by 1945 the authorities decided that there was a need for facilities to encourage amateur drama and accordingly converted the pool into an auditorium.

The first production of the Civic Playhouse as it was called took place on 9th April 1945, performed by local groups. It was G.B.Shaw's *Arms and the Man* and apparently he was impressed enough to send one of his famous postcards in congratulation.

Despite a fire in 1950 necessitating closure for 5 months and in 1957 withdrawal of municipal funding, the Playhouse continued to function. A Theatre and Arts Club was formed, volunteers from the many societies using the premises running the various operations both backstage and front of house.

Outwardly little has changed since 1806, though the tall chimney stack has gone, and the Borough **coat of arms** has been added over the central doorway. Inside, the foyer retains its Edwardian character, and there are the tiles on the bottom of the swimming pool still underneath the auditorium floor!

POETS

Cheltenham has been home, albeit sometimes temporarily, to a number of writers. Many of these have become familiar enough, and their residence marked by plaques. Such names as **Tennyson**, Flecker, whose father was headmaster of **Dean Close School, Dobell** and C.Day Lewis are paralleled by others less well known. Frederick Myers was a pupil at **Cheltenham College** and has a fine memorial in the chapel, though some would argue that his poem *St Paul* serves his memory as much. Then there's Thomas Campbell who wrote magical poems like *Hohenlinden* and rousing pieces such as *Ye Mariners of England*, but so far as Cheltenham is concerned he should be remembered as the biographer of Sarah Siddons, for her **theatre** career virtually began in this town.

POPULATION

Until the first national census in 1801, accurate estimates for the population of Cheltenham, and, indeed, of anywhere, are often hard to come by. Even so, it is possible to gain some impression of the size of Cheltenham over the centuries, as a measure of the town's growth and development.

At the time of Domesday Book, in 1086, for instance, the adult male population of Cheltenham Hundred (a rather larger area than the present town) has been estimated at only 114, while even as late as 1712, when Sir Robert Atkyns included population figures in his *Ancient and Present State of Gloucestershire*, Cheltenham had only an estimated 1500 inhabitants and 321 houses.

By 1712, however, Cheltenham was of the eve of its new role as a spa, and although the latter's impact on the town's population was slow at first, it soon quickened pace. Cheltenham's first **guide book**, published in 1781, gave a figure of 2000 people, while the 1801 census recorded 3076 people in the town. By 1851, that figure had increased tenfold, to 35,051, making it the largest town in the county, and during the 1820s, Cheltenham's rate of population growth had been one of the highest in the provinces. Although many of the new inhabitants were from the wealthy, leisured classes (including, of course, increasing numbers of families with military connections), a larger number were working people who came into the town in search of employment in service, building, manufacture and retail.

After 1851, with the gradual decline of the **spas**, the rate of growth slowed appreciably, and during the first twenty years of this century, when the town's fortunes were at a particularly low ebb, its total population actually declined. Since the 1920s, however, with the gradual revival of the town's economy, its population has grown once more. Barely 50,000 in 1931, it had reached 62,850 by 1951, and continued to grow rapidly, particularly as the Borough's boundaries were extended, in 1974 and again in 1991. As at 1 April 1991, following the most recent boundary change, which brought **Prestbury, Swindon Village**, Up Hatherley and the Reddings into the Borough, the total population stands at around 103,000.

PRESTBURY

Perhaps the most distinctive of all the villages adjoining Cheltenham, Prestbury was made part of Cheltenham Borough in 1991, following a boundary change. It contains a good medieval church and an array of attractive houses and pubs, particularly in its finest street, the Burgage, which represents the old Market Place, from when Prestbury was a small market town. Prestbury also figures large in the history of **horse racing**, including within its boundaries the Cheltenham Racecourse and the childhood home of the champion jockey, Fred **Archer**. It was also a popular resort for Cheltenham's visitors during the 19th century, and boasted its 'Grotto Tea Gardens' and even, for a time, a small spa of its own, the Hyde Spa at what is now Hyde Farm, in the west of the parish. It also has a long-standing reputation as one of the most haunted villages in England!

PROMENADE

Cheltenham's most famous thoroughfare had its origins in the 1790s, when a row of shops, known as the Colonnade, was built on the south side of the **High Street**, where that street now joins 'the Prom', as it is so often called. The Colonnade ran south from the High Street, and although only six shops were built during 1791-4, the intention was to continue its line southwards for around a thousand feet. That, however, had to wait another 20 years, for it was not until 1817-18, with the establishment of the **Imperial Spa** on the site now occupied by the **Queen's Hotel**, that its continuation took place, as a gravelled and tree-lined 'ride' connecting the new spa to the High Street, and known as the Imperial or Sherborne Promenade.

Soon, however, the nature of the tree-lined 'ride' began to change. As early as 1823, with demand for building land and houses at its height in Cheltenham, land on its west side was sold for building development, and soon the fine terraces now occupied by **Hoopers** and by the **Municipal Offices** were built - the first a hotel and the second as private houses. Also built as private houses from around 1825 onwards were a succession of villas on the east side of the Promenade, and it was these that were gradually converted for use as shops, the earliest (1826) being a draper's business known even then as **Cavendish House**. During the early 1830s, further houses were built at the south end of the Prom, opposite **Imperial Square**, and by then the street was the heart of fashionable Cheltenham, the great thoroughfare that chanelled traffic from the High Street towards the fast-growing southern quarters of **Montpellier, Lansdown, Bayshill, Suffolk Square** and **The Park.**

The Promenade has remained the focus of Cheltenham's fashionable shopping ever since, earning for itself earlier this century the title of 'the Bond Street of the West'. Certainly several of its businesses date back to the last century, most notably Cavendish House and **Martin's** the jewellers, while despite modern shop fronts, many of the old Promenade villas survive, particularly above first floor level - this is definitely a street in which to look up! And although many of its trees have been lost in recent years, it still recalls its origins, sweeping towards the Queens Hotel, passing many features of interest, most notably the **Neptune Fountain** and **Royscot House.**

Linden Cottage, Prestbury

Paragon Parade

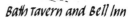

Bath Tavern and Bell Inn

The
Queens
Hotel

PUBLIC HOUSES

Cheltenham **High Street** used to have innumerable inns and brew-houses, typically occupying a strip of land having only a narrow street frontage with an inn yard extending rearwards. Of the few that survive, at the east and west extremities of the High Street, there are only two names which were recorded trading as early as 1820: the Shakespeare Inn, No.386, and the Old Swan, No.37. To these need to be added the Exmouth Arms, Bath Road, established soon after 1816.

Pubs have now been displaced from the High Street's central shopping area; exceptions are the Star Hotel, Regent Street which is pre-Victorian, and Copperfields on Church Street, which has recently altered its 1820 name (the Eight Bells), but is now the nearest approximation to a pub up a High Street alley.

Some interesting pub facades are the tiled Cooper's Arms, 47 High Street, St James' Hotel, Ambrose Street, the Mitre Inn, commanding its small artisan district around Sandford Street, and the Beehive Inn in Montpellier Villas.

Next-door pubs are the Bath Tavern and the Bell Inn in Bath Road and the Compasses Inn and the Welsh Harp in New Street.

Cheltenham pub names were generally predictable, although there were some unusual ones, but no longer trading: the Dove and Rainbow; the Lamb and Flag; the Prince's Plume; and Noah's Ark (not changed much, at 50 St George's Street).

PUBLIC LIBRARY

Cheltenham's imposing late Victorian Public Library was built on the north side of **Clarence Street** (on the site of part of a Regency Terrace called Bedford Buildings) in 1887-9, and was designed by W.H.**Knight.**

Originally, the building served both as a Free Library (as opposed to a private or subscription library, of which the town already had several), and as the Schools of Art and Science, which occupied as its studios the large rooms on the first floor of the building. These rooms were later (and still are) occupied by the town's Museum, which opened in 1907, two years after the Schools moved out to new premises in St Margaret's Road.

Appropriately for such a literary institution, the Library boasts a statue of Shakespeare atop its pedimented front - now, alas, minus his pen, which was lost during restoration work some years ago!

QUAKER BURIAL GROUND

Amongst Cheltenham's oldest 'sights' is the blocked-up doorway of the old Quaker Burial Ground in Grove Street, off the Lower High Street, which bears the date 1700. Now used as a builder's yard, the Burial Ground recalls the town's thriving Quaker congregation which was in existence by at least 1660. They had a small meeting house in Manchester Walk (now part of **Clarence Street**) from 1702 onwards, and the Quaker Meeting House of 1835-6 still survives as part of the **Cheltenham and Gloucester College of Higher Education**'s Shaftesbury Hall campus.

Amongst the congregation during the 18th century was William Mason, who owned the field in which the first spa waters were discovered, and whose daughter, Elizabeth's, marriage to Henry **Skillicorne** had such an important influence on the development of Cheltenham as a spa. She was buried in the Quaker Burial Ground in 1779.

QUEEN'S HOTEL

Since 1838 the town's **Promenade** has had as its focus the Queen's Hotel. Built on the site of the Sherborne or **Imperial Spa**, which had to be moved, its cost was £47,000. The **Jearrad** brothers designed it, modelling the classical capitals of its massive facade on those of the Temple of Jupiter in Rome. When the hotel opened on 21 July, Richard Liddell, from the Clarence Hotel, now **John Dower House**, became its first lessee, paying £2,100 a year. However, despite such generous accommodation as 25 sitting rooms, coffee and billiard rooms, apartments for servants as well as over 70 bedrooms the enterprise did not prosper, and in 1852 the hotel was sold for a mere £8,400. Improvements quickly followed and in 1900 for example provision was made for amateur photographers amongst the guests by installing a dark room.

Many guests of distinction in all walks of life have been to the Queen's: Edward VII when Prince of Wales, Prince Louis Jerome Napoleon and the Rajah of Sarawak; the explorer Nansen, violinist Sarasate, Paderewski, Elgar, Conan Doyle, General **Napier**, and many more. During the Second World War an American Services Club was here, so such personalities as Bob Hope were visitors, and more recently in 1990 the Conservative Central Council meeting in the **Town Hall** saw the hotel hosting a Prime Minister and 5 Cabinet members.

Outside the main entrance stands one of a pair of plinths on which guns captured at Sebastopol were once mounted till the wartime 'salvage drive' removed them, but, more fortunately, to the side of the hotel two lamp standards have survived, reminders of the gas lighting which once had to be privately provided.

RAILWAYS

For a Spa town, visitors are its lifeblood, and so the inhabitants of Cheltenham quickly saw the benefits of rail travel. The stage-coach proprietors, who would ultimately be put out of business by the railway, advertised connections with the Great Western Railway, and offered ever quicker journeys to London.

The opening of the Gloucester and Cheltenham Tramroad in 1810 illustrated the advantages of a railway: it was a 3'6" guage plateway built to carry coal and roadstone from Gloucester Docks, and to 'export' **Leckhampton** stone. Plans for a line to London via Burford and Tring were before Parliament in 1837, but were defeated, and the first main-line railway to reach Cheltenham was the Birmingham and Gloucester Railway which began its service between Cheltenham and Bromsgrove on 24 June 1840. Later in 1840 the railway was extended to Gloucester, over the line to be shared with the Cheltenham and Great Western Railway Union. This company had been established in 1835, but almost spent itself in opposing the Tring Railway and took four years to complete sixteen miles of track between Kemble and Stroud. It was then taken over by the Great Western Railway, and reached the site of St James's Station in 1847. Later St James's Station was to be the departure point for the Cheltenham Flyer, which after a record-breaking journey on 9 July 1923, was for some years the world's fastest timetabled train, admittedly only between Swindon and London (Paddington).

In 1881 the Cheltenham and Banbury Direct Railway, via Leckhampton and Andoversford was opened, and in 1891 the opening of the Midland and South-Western Junction Railway enabled through trains to be run to Southampton. The last of Cheltenham's railways was the Honeybourne line, opened in 1906 to provide the GWR with its own line between Birmingham and the South-West.

Originally through trains on the GWR stopped at St James's Station though as this was a terminus the need to couple a new locomotive and uncouple the original engine caused delay. To avoid this Malvern Road station was built, allowing trains to stop at Cheltenham without having to 'reverse', and later Cheltenham Racecourse Station was built.

By 1970 only Lansdown Station, now stripped of its portico, remained open, offering services on the main South-West - North-East line to Bristol and Birmingham, and stations beyond, and Western Region services to Swindon, with a few through services to London. Of the other lines few buildings remain, but their routes can be traced by cuttings, embankments and bridges; part of the Honeybourne line is a cyclepath. Ironically it is the Gloucester and Cheltenham Tramroad, which closed in 1861, which has had the greatest impact on the townscape; the Gasworks in Gloucester Road were built close to its terminus, much of its route can be traced by the unusually broad pavements and the alignment of certain streets, and the course which it took to Staverton determined the route of the former A 40 (now B 4063) main road to Gloucester.

REGENT ARCADE

Cheltenham's largest and most prestigious new shopping mall, the £23 million Regent Arcade, is built on the site of the historic Plough Hotel, an establishment which, according to George **Rowe**, 'has ever been identified with the early history of Cheltenham; from the humble country inn it has risen through successive stages of improvement'. What Rowe calls its 'rather formidable frontage' may still be identified because after an unsuccessful attempt to retain the hotel's facade, the developers provided an approximate echo.

Designed by Roger Dyer Associates of Cheltenham, the Arcade covers 185,000 square feet and has a total of 78 shops, plus a car park for 540 cars. It was built between 1982 and 1984, and was officially opened by HRH The Princess Royal in May 1985.

The Arcade contains several features of interest, most notably the 'Wishing Fish Clock' which since its installation in 1987 nevers fails to attract spectators. It was designed by Gloucestershire-based artist Kit Williams, the author of the enigmatic book, *Masquerade*, and its mechanism is by the Cheltenham clockmakers, Sinclair Harding & Co. The 45 foot high clock, which cost £80,000, was unveiled in January 1987, and is believed to be the world's tallest mechanical clock, weighing no less than 3 tons. It features a giant white duck, which lays a stream of golden eggs into a box with doors, out of which pop mice and a snake. A sun revolves around a clock face, which is painted with animals, and suspended below the clock is a fish which wiggles its tail, rolls its eyes and plays a tune before producing bubbles from its mouth to the delight of onlookers!

Other features of the Arcade are a Victorian mosaic, depicting a plough team, which once formed part of the entrance to the Plough Hotel, and a Royal coat of arms from the 'Old Town Hall', an early 19th century building which stood in the Plough Yard, and which served in turn as a riding school, a Baptist Chapel and as Cheltenham's first Town Hall. It was demolished to make way for the Arcade, as was the old Regent Motors Garage, where Frank Whittle assembled Britain's first jet engine during 1940-41. The engine was fitted to a Gloster 28/39 and made its maiden flight from Moreton Valence airfield on 15 May 1941; a small commemorative model of the E28/39 stands at the heart of the Arcade to recall the connection.

REGENT HALL

At the north end of Regent Street, not far from the **High Street**, is an attractive former Nonconformist Chapel, now occupied by an estate agent. Built in about 1840 by the Association Methodists, it was originally known as Bethany Chapel, and later as Regent Chapel, though interestingly when the doors were stripped a few years ago the words 'Billiard Rooms'

Cheltenham Spa railway station

St George's Hall, High Street

St Anne's, Pittville Circus Road

revealed themselves!

Regent Street itself is of interest as the site of one of Cheltenham's earliest pleasure grounds, the Regent Gardens, which were opened in about 1810 and were the site of many fetes and events before the opening of the much larger **Montpellier, Imperial** and **Pittville** Gardens.

RICHARDSON, RALPH

Although he lived on Cheltenham only a short time after his birth on 19 December 1902 at 11 **Tivoli Road**, the actor Sir Ralph Richardson remembered with affection climbing into the chestnut tree by the front gate and startling old ladies with a disembodied 'Good Morning' as they walked by. The dignified early 19th century villa was also the home from 1927 until her death in 1941 of Dame Sidney Browne, first president of the College of Nursing. There is no plaque to her, but Sir Ralph came on 6 November 1982, shortly before he died in 1983, to unveil one to himself, when he recounted his childhood memories. Another memorial to him is the Richardson Studio at the **Everyman Theatre**.

ROAD TRANSPORT

Like most small market towns, the Cheltenham of the pre-spa era was virtually isolated by poor roads and a lack of transport facilities to and from the town. In 1738, the inappropriately-named 'Gloucester Flying Machine' took three days to reach London, passengers to and from Cheltenham having to go by private post-chaise either to Gloucester or to Andoversford, on the London Road. Gradually, however, the situation improved, and by 1776, another coach, the 'Old Hereford', did the journey direct from Cheltenham in 26 hours. By the 1820s, when the spa town was in its heyday, the journey time to London had been cut to 10.5 hours; 30 to 40 coaches passed through Cheltenham in all directions each day, coming and going at the various coaching inns, notably the Plough, which was said to have been one of the largest posting-houses outside London.

Although the importance of the coaches declined with the coming of the railways, they never vanished from the transport scene, and in our own century, Cheltenham regained for a while its former importance as a transport hub, as a centre for the National coach network. In 1926, George Readings had established his 'Black and White Coach Company', offering scenic tours of the area, and he soon expanded his activities to include regular services to London and elsewhere. In 1931, he acquired St Margarets, Katherine **Monson**'s former mansion in St Margaret's Road, as a coach station, and until 1984, the coach station was one of England's largest interchanges, the afternoon 'exodus' of coaches at 2.30 pm being a sight to behold, and a cause of great congestion in the town centre! Now, however, that role has gone. Far fewer coaches come to the town and the former coach station awaits redevelopment.

Within the town itself, the need for public transport was minimal during the 18th century - even so, a couple of sedan chairs were available to carry less active visitors between their lodgings and the spa well or **Assembly Rooms**, at 6d a ride, while a system of hand-or horse-drawn 'flys', and hackney carriages developed during the early 19th century. Horses also provided the motive power for Cheltenham's first buses, which ran from 1890 until they were gradually replaced by trams in 1901-3, operated by the Cheltenham Light Railway Company. They in turn were replaced by motor buses from 1912 onwards, and by 1931 the trams had been phased out completely, and the basis of the town's present-day bus system was in place.

RODNEY LODGE

Rodney Road joins the **High Street** where the **Assembly Rooms** used to stand. They were built by Thomas Hughes in 1784 when he had purchased the Powers Court Estate. Though they have been superseded by one of the **Banks**, there is still a reminder of the Hughes family fortune in the elegant Rodney Lodge just to the south. This was built by Thomas's son Robert on what was then called Engine House Lane. Its generous eaves, elegant bow fronted garden facade and the classical porch which straddles the pavement mark it out as one of Cheltenham's important Regency houses. Indeed when it was sold some years later this was the description: 'Rodney Lodge, lately in the occupation of the Earl of Ailesbury, the Marquis of Ormonde and the Earl of Coventry and lastly the Conde de Funchal; with the shrubbery ground, fruit garden, stable and meadow containing 3 acres, a paddock with groups of forest trees bounded by the Chelt in which there is an ancient Right of Fishery ..... altogether a possession not to be equalled in Cheltenham'.

Today those grounds have been drastically reduced but it is still possible to gauge their extent by the fact the the terrace along Rodney Road when built on that land was set back so as not to spoil the view down to the river, which now flows underground anyway!

ROWE, GEORGE

Among the town's most prominent citizens during the early 19th century was the Exeter-born artist and lithographer, George Rowe, who lived in Cheltenham from 1832 to 1852, when he emigrated to Australia to seek his fortune at the gold fields.

While in Cheltenham, Rowe became involved in many aspects of the town's life. He was co-proprietor of one of its **newspapers**, the staunchly Liberal *Cheltenham Examiner*, co-proprietor of the **Royal Well,** a member of the **Town Commissioners,** and, in 1846-7, High Bailiff of Cheltenham, a

Victorian equivalent of the present Mayor.

His main claim to fame, however, was as a print maker, and he published literally hundreds of views of the British Isles, including many of Cheltenham and Gloucestershire, which were bought by tourists and which are still avidly collected today. It is to Rowe that we owe many of the fine images of the early Victorian town that are available to us.

The later years of Rowe's life, following his journey to Australia, were perhaps the most remarkable of all. After a short time as a gold prospector, Rowe turned back to painting, and made a living painting and selling views of the goldfields and the settlers. He returned to England in 1859 and settled at Exeter, where he produced a series of fine oil paintings of Australian scenes, which won him a medal at the 1862 London International Exhibition, two years before his death. Because of these and his other Australian paintings, he is still remembered in that country as one of the leading artists of the gold rush.

While in Cheltenham, Rowe had a number of homes, one of which, 2 Priory Terrace, off London Road, where he and his family lived in 1832-5, now has a commemorative plaque.

ROYAL CRESCENT

Cheltenham's earliest block of Regency houses was begun in 1805-6 on the west side of Church Meadow, the field across which ran the path between the town and the **Royal Well**. The Crescent was developed by Joseph **Pitt**, for whom it was designed by a prominent Bath architect, Charles Harcourt Masters. The houses were intended to provide fashionable lodgings for visitors to the spa, of which there was a distinct lack in the early years of the 19th century.

Originally, it seems, the plan was for two blocks of 12 houses with a roadway between, not unlike the great Circus at Bath, but on a smaller scale. However, as was so often the case with Cheltenham's ambitious building developments, theory was not translated into reality: by 1812, only 12 houses had been built, and during the next decade, the development was completed as a crescent of just 18 houses, all of which were in place by 1825.

Even so, Royal Crescent remains one of Cheltenham's great architectural 'set-pieces', despite its facade being screened by trees, and the presence opposite it of the unattractive Royal Well Bus Station. Built of brick with stuccoed facades, the houses are particularly noteworthy for their contemporary **ironwork** balconies and railings, provided by John Bradley of Worcester - note in particular the fine oil lamp holders outside Nos 9 and 10.

Royal Crescent housed many notable men and women throughout the town's heyday, including Dr **Boisragon**, who lived at No 11, and the Duke of Gloucester, **George III**'s nephew, who spent many seasons at No 18 between about 1825 and his death in 1834. It was here that he was visited, in 1830, by his cousin, the Duchess of Kent and her young daughter, Princess Victoria - the future Queen's one and only visit to Cheltenham.

ROYAL WELL
The name of Cheltenham's unprepossessing town centre bus station, and of Royal Well Place, a rather more attractive short street nearby, are reminders of Cheltenham's earliest and most historic spa well, at which **George III** drank the Cheltenham waters in 1788. The Royal Well (also known at one time or another as the Old Well, the Original Well, or the King's Well) stood on what is now the site of the Princess Hall of **Cheltenham Ladies' College**. Between the discovery of the medicinal spring in about 1716, and the coming to Cheltenham of Captain Henry **Skillicorne** in 1738, it was a fenced enclosure with a thatched hut above. Then, between 1738 and 1742, Skillicorne deepened the spring to form a proper well, installed a pumping system so that the waters might be more easily obtained, and built a brick Pump Room above, with a small assembly room to one side. About 30 years later, Skillicorne's son William added a new 'Long Room' to one side of the existing buildings, and the old assembly room was converted for use as lodging for the 'pumper', the lady who was employed to dispense the waters to the subscribers, and as a small manufactory for bottling the waters for sale. Later, it served as a 'fancy repository', selling prints, china and other souvenirs to the visitors.

The other notable feature of the Royal Well was the **Well Walk,** which connected it to the town, while to the south of the Well, the so-called Serpentine Walk led to Grove Cottage, the residence for many years of Sir Charles Morgan, one of the town's leading military figures. The land around the Well was laid out as gardens.

The Skillicornes' Royal Well buildings survived until 1849, when they were demolished to make way for a much larger and grander Pump Room, designed by Samuel Onley in the Corinthian style; in its day, its ballroom was the largest room in the county, and the building served as both a pump room and as a Theatre and Music Hall. Despite the declining popularity of the waters, the new Royal Well and its adjoining gardens formed one of the town's social foci for a quarter of a century, and were the site of many great events, including some of the largest flower shows ever held in the provinces, and of the great Cheltenham 1854 Exhibition of the Works of Art and Science, for which a large glass and steel 'Crystal Palace' was built in the gardens, only to be dismantled after the event was over!

Eventually, however, the use of the building changed, with the changing nature of the town, and it is fitting that in 1876 the Royal Well building was acquired as an examination hall by the Cheltenham Ladies'

College. It continued in use until 1897, when it was demolished to make way for the Princess Hall, beneath whose floor the site of Cheltenham's historic beginnings as a spa survives.

ROYSCOT HOUSE
One of the most prominent buildings in the **Promenade** is the new office building on the corner of St George's Road, occupied by the Royscot Trust Finance Group, part of the Royal Bank of Scotland.

The building, which adjoins the terrace which includes the **Municipal Offices**, is built on the site to which the 1817 **Imperial Spa** was relocated in 1837, following its removal to make way for the **Queen's Hotel**. The former spa building then served as a warehouse for a century before being demolished to make way for a **cinema** in 1937. The cinema was itself demolished in 1985, and the new office block - one of the most successful fusions of old and new in Cheltenham - was built, in 1985-7 at a cost of £3 million, by a local firm of developers and builders, Britannia Ltd. It was designed by the Stroud-based Falconer Partnership.

ST ANDREW'S UNITED REFORMED CHURCH
This large stone-built church, with its prominent tower and spire, stands at the junction of Montpellier Street and Fauconberg Road, opposite the **Cheltenham Ladies' College**. It was originally built for the Presbyterian congregation that had previously worshipped at the former **Cheltenham Chapel** in **St George's Square**.

ST ANNE'S
Reputedly the most haunted house in Cheltenham, St Anne's in Pittville Circus Road was built by Henry Swinhoe in 1860. Apparently he degenerated into an alcoholic, leading his second wife Imogen the same way. It was after the couple died that sightings of a tall woman dressed as a widow were reported.

During the following ten years when the house had been rented by the family of a Captain Despard the ghostly figure appeared in many rooms and even in the garden where the children accepted her to the extent of playing round her figure.

The house's subsequent history has been that of a private school, Diocesan Retreat, and now flats. Perhaps the ghost has been overwhelmed by these changes, for occupants today seem to be unaware of it.

ST GEORGE'S HALL
252 **High Street** is a stationer's shop, but above its windows there is a panel describing it as St George's Hall. On 19 April 1856 a local newspaper announced its opening as a place for functions not large enough to justify

use of the Town Hall in Regent Street. The first event to be held was an exhibition, described as a working model of the Crimea - the war had been over only 2 months.

Since then the Hall has been host to a wide range of activities: Red Cross training in the 1930s, previews of sculptures for the Montreal Expo in the 1960s. The Plymouth Brethren used it for their meetings in the 1940s just as the Anglicans had done a century earlier whilst **St Matthew's** was being built.

Today it has been thoroughly restored, though there might well not have been much to save. It was found that for years the gas supply had been left on, only newspapers stuffed in the pipe preventing an explosion!

ST GEORGE'S PLACE

One of Cheltenham's oldest and most historic streets, St George's Place runs southwards from the **High Street** towards **Clarence Street** and the **Bayshill Estate**. Originally known as Stills Lane, the street seems to have originated as a lane leading towards the original spa well, on the site of the **Cheltenham Ladies' College**. Its earliest surviving buildings are a row of brick and stucco houses on its eastern side, (16-18 St George's Place), which are all that is left of a terrace of four houses built in 1788-89 and called St George's Place, a name that was later given to the entire street. One of the houses, now demolished, was the home of Edward **Jenner**. The street contains a number of other attractive houses, several of which are undergoing restoration. These include those in Chapel Walk, which leads to the former **Cheltenham Chapel**. St George's Place also contains the birthplace of the champion jockey, Fred **Archer**, the large red-brick Shaftesbury Hall and, facing St James's Square, the elaborate former Locke's Bakery.

ST GEORGE'S SQUARE

Laid out from about 1806 onwards on a field called 'Rack Close' at the west end of the **High Street**, St George's Square was altered out of all recognition when Ambrose Street was cut through it. Even so, the Square still retains a number of attractive Regency houses on its south side, along with Cheltenham's earliest surviving Nonconformist chapel, the former **Cheltenham Chapel** (now an office building) on its east side, overlooking the well-manicured Bowling Green.

ST GREGORY'S ROMAN CATHOLIC CHURCH

The imposing tower and spire of the Roman Catholic priory church of St Gregory is a prominent landmark on Cheltenham's skyline, particularly at night, when it is floodlit. The church was begun in 1854, in the 'Decorated Gothic' style of the 14th century, and was built in stages between then and

Wynnstay House, formerly
St James's Square Infants School

St Paul's church

St Mary's
church

1876. Its architect was Charles Hansom of Clifton.

The church replaced a smaller chapel of 1809-10 on the same site, and its size is an indication of Cheltenham's large Catholic population, which traces back to the years of the Napoleonic Wars, when Cheltenham was a popular refuge for French exiles.

ST JAMES'S CHURCH

Suffolk Square's noble terraces have at one corner a perfect complement to the classical facades, with the Gothic west end of a church designed by Edward Jenkins, a young local architect. However, either his courage failed him when it came to spanning the roof, or the church authorities lost confidence in him, for J.B.**Papworth** was called in to complete the building in 1830. Perhaps Jenkins's elopement four years earlier with Charlotte Balfour, daughter of one of the Church's council, had something to do with it.

The interior has been given a false ceiling though it is still possible to see the elaborate roof which gave Jenkins so much trouble. As it is no longer used for services the walls are covered but, behind the curtaining, monuments remain. One depicts a young officer's death at the siege of Sebastopol, another records that butt of parodists the playwright, 'popular author and accomplished gentleman', Nathaniel Thomas Haynes Bayly, who died in 1839 having given the world the memorable lyric, *I'd be a butterfly*.

ST JAMES'S SQUARE

Although not actually a square at all - rather two roads at right angles to each other - St James's Square contains a number of interesting and attractive buildings. These include the former home of Lord **Tennyson**, the **Synagogue** and Britain's earliest surviving **Infant School**, opposite which stands one of the town's most attractive brick buildings, the small Fire Station of 1906. Also in the Square are two of Cheltenham's modern new office blocks - the Mercantile and General Reinsurance Company, occupying the site of the Great Western Railway's St James's Square Station, opened in 1847 and closed in 1966, and the new joint headquarters of the Universities Central Council on Admissions and the Polytechnics Clearing House. The latter stands in the centre of a large car park, which occupies the site of one of 19th century Cheltenham's most unusual features, the 20 acre Jessop's Nurseries, a commercial nursery ground that was also open to visitors and which comprised walks, shrubberies, greenhouses, hothouses, an aviary and a small zoological collection. Once a popular attraction with visitors, it has long since vanished.

Also long since vanished is Cheltenham's one archaeological mystery - the so-called St James's Square long barrow or 'knapp' (the latter name being recalled by the nearby Knapp Road). Believed to have been a prehistoric burial chamber, it stood close to the former Infant School and was opened in 1832, its stones later being used for a cider press at nearby Knapp House! What has survived is the curved wall marking the railway locomotive turntable.

ST JAMES'S SQUARE INFANTS SCHOOL
It is the oldest surviving infants' school building in the country, having been opened in July 1830. Its 60ft school room has been extended but the long windows are original, and the playground, one of the first to be equipped with swings and climbing apparatus, attracted in those early years members of the public who found it an education to observe for an hour each day the activities of children. That such a school came into being must be attributed to the pioneer Samuel **Wilderspin** who himself lived in Alpha House, St George's Road, and inevitably to Francis **Close**, whose support for the enterprise extended to raising £1,200 towards its cost.

For some years the building served as a sorting office, and then as a printers. Today its name is Wynnstay House and its function that of offices.

ST JOHN'S LODGE, TIVOLI
In 1845 part of a field called Marybone Park was sold, and the present St John's Lodge built on the plot which had been the Tivoli Nursery. Its southern boundary was the railway that brought stone from **Leckhampton** quarries, and it faced westwards along what was then known as Lippiate Street, though today it is the A40.

Many occupants have lived in this impressive stone faced house with its scrolls on the parapet and strange 'sausage-rolls' decoration under the cornice. In 1891, Miss C.E.Sturt is named, a relative of Charles **Sturt** who had been in nearby **Tivoli Road** some years earlier. But the most poignant resident was Prince Caulker. He had been brought to England in 1853 under the patronage of the Countess of Huntingdon's Missionary Society, from West Africa. During his 6 year stay he not only lost his father Camar Bar, the King of Bompey, his mother and his throne, but also his sight. St John's Lodge could not have been a happy address for him.

ST LUKE'S CHURCH
St Luke's, in College Road, was built in 1853-4, both as a place of worship for the Sandford area and to serve as a chapel for **Cheltenham College**. It was designed by a London architect, Frederick Ordish, and its architectural style may be said to mark a transition from the rather light 'Regency' Gothic of **Holy Trinity** and **Christ Church** to the heavier Victorian Gothic that reached its apogee in Cheltenham in the work of John **Middleton**.

ST MARGARET'S TERRACE

St Margaret's Terrace, on the north side of the Northern Relief Road, is one of the most imposing terraces in Cheltenham, and is particularly unusual in that care and attention was clearly given to the rear elevation as well as to the facade. Built by the Hon. Katherine **Monson** in 1820-5, it comprises six stone-fronted houses, each with good examples of ornamental ironwork. Once the homes of large Victorian households, the houses have more recently (1981) been well restored and converted into flats by the Cheltenham and District Housing Association.

ST MARK'S CHURCH

The earliest of John **Middleton**'s five Cheltenham churches, St Mark's was begun in 1860 and has the distinction of being the only one of Middleton's churches that was completed as originally intended. Like Middleton's other churches, it was designed so that it could be built in stages, as funds permitted. The nave and chancel were built by 1861, so that the church could be used while the money for the tower and spire was raised. That had been achieved, and the spire completed, by the end of 1866. The transepts were added in the 1880s.

Although some way from the town's historic centre, the area around St Mark's church is not without interest. Centred on the Lansdown Railway Station, it includes a number of attractive houses of 1860 onwards, particularly in Church Road. Historically, the area, known originally as the Libertus Estate, is of interest in that it was developed by the Cheltenham and Gloucester Freehold Land Society, which was established by local Liberals in 1850 in order to secure for its supporters enough freehold land to enable them to vote in Parliamentary elections!

ST MARY'S CHURCH

Standing in the centre of town, the parish church has much of Cheltenham's history written in its fabric. Architecturally it dates from the 12th century with the arches under its central tower, and has something to show of each succeeding century. Its superb circular rose window has the tracery on the tilt, while many other windows have rich flowing designs mainly 14th century in origin. Other rewarding features include a stone vaulted north porch, a canopied piscina, and fine stained glass by amongst others Heaton & Butler, Hardman, and Clayton & Bell. Appropriately the Royal Arms are those of **George III**, though the box pews and galleries, once filled by congregations eager to hear the sermons of Francis **Close**, have gone. Of the many memorials abounding on the walls that to Henry **Skillicorne** exceeds all others in its lengthy description of his career and achievements. Other inscriptions worth investigating are that to Katherine a'Court, under the rose window, and John English's tribute to his wife, in the south aisle.

The churchyard path on the south side still has set in it brass measuring marks where lengths of rope or cloth could be checked. Also in the churchyard is what remains of the town's medieval churchyard cross, along with examples of the 'dragon and onion' lampstandards. There is amongst the tombstones one commemorating a pig-killer called Higgs!

ST MATTHEW'S CHURCH
A town centre church in Clarence Street and almost within singing distance of **St Mary's**, it was built in 1879. Ewan Christian designed it, providing a fine chancel, owing something to French architecture. Even though it has lost its spire and much of its tower, taken down in 1952 and 1972 respectively, the sense of spaciousness inside makes it a fitting choice year by year for the town's civic services.

ST PAULS
Named after the Greek Revival St Paul's Church that stands at its heart, the St Pauls area, to the west of the town centre, forms an area of small, mainly red-brick artisan housing, which still retains the scale of the mid-19th century.

The oldest of the streets are those leading off the Lower High Street, many of which date from the very early years of the 19th century, following the inclosure of the Open Fields. Among them, the former Rutland Street (now the southern half of Brunswick Street) retains several restored cottages of about 1806-10. Other attractive corners are the narrow Malthouse Lane, Larput Place, with some good ironwork, and above all, St Paul's Street North, whose stuccoed houses all date from 1834-6. An unusual feature of St Paul's Street North is the way in which an attempt has been made to align the new street to the facade of St Paul's Church - it has not, however, succeeded, because the field in which the street was built was too far to the west of the church, a good example of how the developing townscape was dictated by the existing pattern of fields!

Just to the west of St Paul's Street North is the narrow St Paul's Lane, by the original buildings of St Paul's College. This actually follows a field boundary, and the 'curve' of the plough may still be seen in its shape!

ST PAUL'S CHURCH
This classical style building with a columned facade and cupola tower was designed in 1827 by John **Forbes,** for the artisan congregation of this area of the town. Because most of its sittings were free (unlike the fashionable Proprietary Chapels, in which seats had to be paid for) it was often known as the 'Free Church'. Later additions were its north chapel, 1932, stained glass of 1963 and a wrought iron pulpit which pulled out on runners.

Sculpture

Scott-Cooper

Henry
Skillicorne

Former spas: Montpellier
and in
Vittoria
Walk

ST PETER'S CHURCH

In the first half of the 19th century, the Tewkesbury Road area was what today might be called depressed. The parishioners then described it somewhat more forcibly: 'People of respect are afraid to live here because life and property are not safe.....persons are stoned or pelted with mud.....one or two have lost their lives.' So, in 1849, a church designed by S.W.**Daukes** was consecrated here. What influence this passable imitation of a Norman Templars church had on the crime figures cannot be proved, but today its atmosphere and character certainly impress.

SALEM BAPTIST CHAPEL

This imposing Gothic Revival chapel, situated in Clarence Parade at the heart of the Victorian town, has a most impressive window (echoing the fine 14th century tracery in **St Mary's** Church), and what are said to be the tallest chapel doors in England.

The congregation at Salem was originally part of the congregation of Bethel Chapel (now the **Christadelphian Hall**), who seceded in 1835 and met for eight years in the now-demolished Old Town Hall, which stood on part of the site of the new **Regent Arcade**.

Salem Chapel was built in 1843-4 and caused considerable comment when it opened; one local newspaper wrote that 'the florid style of its architecture, and magnificent Gothic window seem particularly to contradict the simplicity and lowliness usually sought to be attached to dissent in this country', while a later writer noted that the chapel 'exhibits an immense advance in the development of architectural taste in connection with the dissenting body'.

The chapel is built of brick, with an ashlar stone facade, and although the interior has undergone considerable alteration, with part of the chapel being separated off for secular use, it is still used regularly by a Baptist congregation.

SCOTT COOPERS

There are very few original shop fronts left in Cheltenham, so it is particularly rewarding to find an example that is virtually unchanged. 52 **Promenade** has been a jewellers' since 1912 when Mr Waldron Scott Cooper opened his business there. He had come from Norwich in 1892 where his father was one of six brothers, all of whom were jewellers.

This shop, a survivor from the age of 'art nouveau', has seen many distinguished customers pass through the doorway with its delightful mermaid handle. Among them have been the grand-daughter of Queen Victoria, Princess Marie Louise, an earlier Duke of Beaufort, and more recently the late Princess Imeretinska of **Tivoli Road**.

SCULPTURE

Setting aside the examples to be seen in the town's churches, there are many visible in its streets which add significance to the view, and provide evidence of Cheltenham's history.

Taking statues first, perhaps the most pertinent is that of Edward **Wilson** in the Long Garden of the **Promenade**. Over £300 was publicly subscribed, and it had appropriately the widow of Captain Scott as designer. R.L.Boulton, a local firm, cast the figure, while its unveiling in 1914 was by a president of the Royal Geographical Society.

Also dating from 1914, and certainly equally conspicuous is the statue of Edward VII in **Montpellier**. Informally dressed in a Norfolk suit, he somewhat sentimentally offers benevolence to a 'ragged' child. The donors, Mr and Mrs Drew of Hatherley Court, were known for work in rescuing old cab horses and seaside donkeys.

Another royal subject, in **Montpellier Gardens**, is a rare portrayal of William IV, in his Garter robes. An inscription states that it was erected in **Imperial Gardens** to mark in 1833 the passing of the Reform Bill - important for Cheltenham's parliamentary representation - and that it was paid for by public subscription, but other records date it 1831, and Thomas Henney the donor. The sculptor is reputed to have been a self taught artist.

Among the statues on the fronts of **Cheltenham Ladies' College**, there is one, facing St George's Road, that symbolises Hope. Apparently the designer H.H.**Martyn** made a mistake with the shape of the anchor. When this was pointed out to him by an admiral living nearby, he had the whole thing re-carved.

There is a representation of Henry **Skillicorne** in the little garden behind the **Town Hall**, placed here in 1963 to mark the bicentenary of his death. P.Braisby, a local man, designed it.

Two other modern examples of sculpture are to be found in the central area: at St James House, on the site of the former railway station is a group of figures symbolising Strength and Energy lifting up Misfortune, this being the work in bronze of David Backhouse in 1978; the other sculptor represented is Barbara Hepworth whose three panels on the former chief office of the **Cheltenham and Gloucester Building Society** in **Clarence Street** date from 1972 and are entitled *Theme and Variations*.

But the most photographed sculpture in the town must surely be the **Neptune Fountain** in the Promenade. Based on the Trevi Fountain in Rome, it was designed by a former Borough Surveyor in 1893 and made by Boulton's. It stands over the culverted **River Chelt**, by the second site of **Imperial Spa**.

SHARPE AND FISHER

It was in 1912 that Mr and Mrs J.C.Fisher opened their ironmongery and hardware shop in Pittville Street. To build up custom Mr Fisher travelled widely around the Cotswold area on horseback, subsequently taking to a bicycle and eventually the train when he extended his visiting as far afield as Wiltshire and the Welsh Border. By the early 1920s the shop was becoming familiar through its sale of 'Spa' fireplaces, and it was not long before the purchase of a builder's yard in Swindon Road enabled it to expand into the supplying of construction materials.

When the Malvern Road station site became vacant because of the closure of the **railway** line, the firm, now Sharpe and Fisher, took it over. Today, large buildings have transformed the place, though close scrutiny of its gates will reveal their 'GWR' origin.

SKILLICORNE, HENRY

Born in the Isle of Man, a sea captain employed by the Elton family of Bristol, Henry Skillicorne met and married Elizabeth, the daughter of William Mason who had retired to that city from Cheltenham. Henry, having now acquired through his wife's inheritance the field in Bayshill which had a well, soon realised the potential value of its water, properties which a Dr Short extolled in his *History of Mineral Waters* in 1740. He set about improving the supply: a brick shelter was built, pumps installed, and access paths provided. Skillicorne also bought up surrounding land.

By all accounts, and his epitaph in **St Mary's** church is of extraordinary length, he was an exceptional person: 'tall, robust, able to speak seven languages, and well acquainted with the world having traded in the Mediterranean, Netherlands and America'.

For 25 years he lived in Cheltenham, supervising its development as a spa, and playing his part in the business of the parish. Strangely there has been little in the way of commemorating his contribution to the town's prosperity, indeed apart from that inscription in the parish church and a modern garden in **Imperial Square** where a portrait bas-relief has been placed, Henry Skillicorne and his well have sunk into obscurity.

SMIRKE, SIR ROBERT

The architect, Sir Robert Smirke, is best remembered for his design of the British Museum portico, the romantic Eastnor Castle near Ledbury, and Shire Hall in Gloucester. In 1851 he retired to live in **Suffolk Square**, at what was then known simply as No 20, dying there in 1867.

Incidentally five years later when Dr Thomas Jex-Blake, Principal of **Cheltenham College**, made it his family home it became Bunwell House, after the Norfolk village where he owned land.

Later it was used as a boarding house by **Cheltenham Ladies' College**, and now it has been made into flats and given the name Montpellier House.

SOUTH TOWN

South Town is the original name for one of Cheltenham's best preserved artisan districts, that jigsaw of side-streets, terraces, chapels, workshops and pubs which is centred on the present Bath Road shops and is enclosed by the green spaciousness of **Cheltenham College, Suffolk Square** and **The Park.**

Fortunately situated a glorious walk's distance from the town centre, up the **Promenade** to **Montpellier Rotunda** and through Suffolk Square and Suffolk Parade, South Town has escaped much of the redevelopment pressure of recent decades, and it was always a more complete, self-contained townlet than the other large artisan districts of Lower End and **Fairview.** Here lived the tradesmen, school-teachers, stone masons, laundresses, coachmen and straw-bonnet makers.

Laying-out started before 1820, in fields alongside the then New Bath Road and the crucial horse-drawn tramroad of 1811, which brought building stone down from **Leckhampton** Hill quarries into stone depots off Great Norwood Street. This Gloucester and Cheltenham Tramroad also brought Forest of Dean coal from Gloucester Docks to coal sidings off Norwood Road, until its route via Westal Green was closed in 1861, and became the present Queen's Road and Andover Road.

At the centre of South Town, the Westal Brook was once joined by the Nolty Brook, before flowing on westwards through the present Hatherley Park. That land around the two brooks remained the only green open space inside South Town when its building was most complete, towards the end of the 19th century. This half-acre of 'town green' was the Exmouth Arms' bowling-green and pleasure ground. The public house itself was re-fronted in 1898 style, but it dates from around 1816, its pub sign still commemorating Admiral Viscount Exmouth's triumphal stay in the spa, for recuperation after his expedition to Algiers to suppress the notorious Barbary pirates.

Many of the shops along Bath Road still show their origin as modest houses with front gardens. Yet they are arranged next to the grandest house in Cheltenham, Thirlestaine House, a private palace, with its art gallery wings embellished with 'Parthenon Frieze'.

Leaving at the south end of Bath Road, a walk down Gratton Road and Great Norwood Street reveals a delightful range of housefronts, plus St Philip and St James' Church (1879), the former St James' School (1865) and Bethesda Chapel (1845). Great Norwood Street then continues back towards **Montpellier Gardens** as Suffolk Parade, which contains South Town's more genteel shops, now largely antiques, and the 'Daffodil', a **cinema** from 1922 until 1963.

Charles
Sturt

Synagogue

Street light standards
near The Queens Hotel

Former antique shop in Montpellier
Avenue owned by Ron Summerfield

SPAS

It is to its spas that the Cheltenham of today owes its size, character and indeed its industry. Before the discovery of a spring whose salt deposits attracted pigeons - hence their appearance on the Borough's **Arms** - and consequent exploitation of the water itself, there was here but another small market town. The waters were first discovered in about 1718, and twenty years later, development began in earnest. A retired sea captain, Henry **Skillicorne**, the owner of the site through marriage, soon had a well dug, a brick structure, and some initial success in attracting those whose lifestyle benefitted from the purgative action of the water. This **Royal Well** as it came to be called has disappeared beneath the **Ladies' College**, though not before it received the Royal Approval from the visit of **George III** in 1788. From then onwards other springs were sought.

Today the oldest spa building is to be found in Vittoria Walk where at Hygeia House, now called Vittoria House, the Liverpool and London banker, Henry Thompson, opened his supply in 1804. Five years later another source was developed in **Montpellier**, its original structure being simply a wooden pavilion. By 1817 the stone building, Montpellier Spa, seen today as Lloyds Bank had been built to the design of G.A.**Underwood**, though the dome, richly decorated on the inside, was not added till 1826, and then by another hand, J.B.**Papworth's**.

Further spas were promoted: the Sherborne or **Imperial Spa** where the **Queen's Hotel** stands, in **Cambray**, at **Alstone**, and above all at **Pittville**.

SPIRAX SARCO

This enigmatically named firm has been an established part of Cheltenham's commercial life since 1945 when it acquired the semi-derelict Charlton House at **Charlton Kings**. The 'Sarco' part derives from a company called Sanders Rehders which imported from Germany, while 'Spirax' was originally the name given to steam traps, used in the USA, employing a spiral design.

Thus the engineering firm grew, today producing such items as temperature controls, pumps, compressed air equipment and heat exchangers.

Charlton House too has a history. Dating from the end of the 18th century, it has been a girls' school, a vicarage, prisoner-of-war camp, the US Army Legal Headquarters, and of course a private house. It was in 1907 that a tragedy occurred when the Podmore family was living here. For the young 14 year old son, Bob, sustained a kick on the head from his horse. The father was out at the time but returned to find the boy dying. By all accounts Bob was an exceptional child and his funeral marked it, with a long procession of firemen, police and indeed the Vine Harriers, for he had been its youthful Master. It is reputedly still a house haunted by Bob's father rushing up the main staircase to his son's room.

SQUARES
Like most fashionable 18th and 19th century towns,Cheltenham had its due share of residential Squares, a classic feature of English town planning at this time. Many of Cheltenham's great open squares in fact began life as 'ornamental pleasure grounds' attached to the spas, and only later became 'urbanised' when houses were built around them: **Imperial Square** is Cheltenham's best example of this. Others were intended from the outset as residential developments, and **Suffolk Square, Clarence Square** and **Wellington Square** - all with suitably aristocratic names - are good examples. Elsewhere, Cheltenham has three squares that are no longer squares at all! Portland Square lost its central open space to later building, while **St George's Square** has been truncated by having Ambrose Street run through it. Oddest of all is **St James's Square**, which comprises two roadways and a large open space, now a car park but once a large nursery ground.

STREET LAMPS
On 28 September 1818 Cheltenham enjoyed for the first time street gas lighting and has a number of interesting and attractive street lamps. The earliest are almost certainly the three oil lamp holders of about 1823 that are mounted on stone pillars outside **Paragon Parade** in Bath Road. Near the entrance to the car park of the **Queen's Hotel** two standards survive, reminders of private provision for street lighting. But perhaps the town's most ornate lampstand is the 'Gordon Lamp', at the busy junction of Lansdown Road, Montpellier Terrace and Lypiatt Road. It was erected in 1887 in memory of General George Gordon, who had been killed at Khartoum, in the Sudan, two years earlier. The lamp has an elaborate base of red and grey Scottish granite, while the lamp standard itself is supported by cherubs and has three lamp-holders.

The Gordon Lamp was designed for gas, but was converted for electricity in 1900, and the introduction of electricity to the town from 1895 onwards led to the appearance of a succession of new lamps of some interest. The best of them are the so-called 'dragon and onion' lamps that were designed by the Borough Surveyor, Joseph Hall, good examples of which may be seen in **St Mary's** churchyard, Crescent Place, Regent Street and Trafalgar Street.

STURT, CHARLES
Born in Bengal in the closing years of the 18th century, Charles Sturt belongs to the history of 19th century exploration in Australia. After serving

as an army officer in Spain, France and Ireland, he found himself in 1827 in Sydney as a major on the staff of Ralph **Darling**. Thus began that memorable series of expeditions with Hume and with Macleay resulting in the discovery and mapping of the Murray Darling river basin. By 1839 he was Surveyor-General of South Australia, Colonial Secretary and Treasurer. In 1853 he returned with his family to England, and ten years later moved into 19 **Clarence Square**, having lived a little while at the now-demolished St Edmunds in **Tivoli Road**. His continued interest in Australian exploration earned him nomination for a knighthood, but unfortunately he died before it could be accorded. His death in 1869 at 19 Clarence Square brought tributes not only to his exploits, his skills in drawing birds and animals, but also, as fellow explorers Eyre and Harrison-Browne put it, his personal qualities which 'enabled him to pursue among savages a path never stained by bloodshed'.

SUFFOLK SQUARE

Once part of the property of the De la Bere family of Southam, the future site of Suffolk Square was purchased in 1808 by the Earl of Suffolk and Berkshire, who built himself a bow-fronted town house known as Galipot Lodge on the site of the 18th century Galipot Farm, now occupied by Suffolk Square flats. Then, in 1820, the Earl resold a large part of his land to James Fisher, proprietor of the Clarence Hotel (now **John Dower House**). Fisher proceeded to lay out a new residential Square, employing a relatively unknown local architect, Edward Jenkins, to design its terraces. Work was underway by the end of 1823, although, in common with many other building estates of the 1820s, such as **Lansdown** and **Pittville**, work was disrupted in the aftermath of the financial and banking crisis of December 1825 onwards. Building in the Square continued for many years, and some of its houses date from as late as 1848, when the superb terrace on its north side was finally completed.

The Square has many fine houses, at one of which, No.20, the architect Robert **Smirke** died in 1867. Also in the Square is the Regency Gothic **St James's** church (now a parish hall), the site of which was donated by James Fisher, which leads one, perhaps irreverently, to wonder if that is why the church's dedication to St James was chosen! The Square's central garden is home to the town's long-established Bowling Club, and when matches are underway, it adds further charm to an already most attractive scene.

SUMMERFIELD, RONALD ERNEST

Cheltenham has for many years boasted a large number of antique shops, particularly in the Montpellier and Suffolk Road areas, and of these the most remarkable was that run by Ronald Summerfield, in Montpellier Avenue from 1952 until his death in 1989.

Born at Derby in 1916, Ronald Summerfield started collecting antiques as a boy, and later opened an antique shop in his native town. In 1952, he moved with his parents to Cheltenham where they bought a house in Bayshill Road, and Ronald opened his Montpellier shop. Collecting, and especially the excitement of the auction room, remained his lifelong passion. His collection grew rapidly, and as he rarely sold anything except to finance further purchases, every room in his shop and house gradually filled with antiques, pictures and books. By the time of his death, his collection approached a million items. Although his collection was most remarkable for its quantity, it also contained much of quality. The combination of a good eye and a very diverse knowledge enabled him to acquire, at low prices, many items that would in later years become fashionable and expensive.

Following his death, his entire collection - apart from a small number of items bequeathed to the **Art Gallery and Museum** - was sold at auction, the sales taking no less than 25 days and comprising over 14,000 lots. In terms of quantity, it was the largest auction sale of a single collection held this century, and attracted considerable media attention. In all, his collection realised almost £8 million, all of which will be put to charitable use - no doubt to the great future benefit of Cheltenham and its inhabitants.

Although Summerfield's is no more, the shop remains, a reminder of one of Cheltenham's eccentric collectors.

SUSSEX HOUSE
Flanked in Winchcombe Street on the one side by Marlborough House, which was for a while a school of Domestic Science, and on the other by Bordeaux House, Sussex House was during World War I a small vegetarian hotel run by a Mrs Gandy. When Judith, daughter of the French novelist Leon Cladel, announced she was going to stay with her sister in Cheltenham, the great sculptor Rodin decided he would accompany her, and bring his mistress, Rose Beuret, too!

So it was to Mrs Gandy's that they came, and it is recorded that the sometimes irascible artist was, during his short stay, 'punctual at breakfast, lunch and tea, preserving the silence and immobility of a statue .

SWINDON VILLAGE
Brought into Cheltenham Borough under a boundary change in 1991, Swindon Village, to the north-west of the town has one feature of considerable interest - the 12th century hexagonal tower of its otherwise rebuilt church, one of only two examples in Gloucestershire of this rare form of tower design. Apart from that, however, the village has been swamped by new light industrial development and has little character.

Also part of Swindon is an area known as Maud's Elm, now covered in

Suffolk
Square

swindon Village

Tennyson's house, St James Square

Thirlestaine Hall

modern housing, but not long ago, semi-rural. The name recalls a popular Cheltenham legend - namely that of a Swindon girl, Maud Bowen, who was buried at a crossroads in Swindon Lane (at its junction with Malvern Street), having been deemed to have committed suicide. As was traditional, an elm stake was driven through her grave, and this eventually grew into a tree 80 feet high! Whether the legend is true is doubtful, but the tree certainly existed - though in 1907 it was struck by lightning and had to be cut down for safety. Near the church is a half timbered dwelling for many years called Maud's Cottage and reputedly the home of the unfortunate girl.

SYNAGOGUE
One of Cheltenham's hidden gems, the Synagogue of 1837-9 stands on the east side of the appropriately-named Synagogue Lane, off **St James's Square**.

The building was designed by an important local architect, W.H.**Knight**, and is virtually unaltered. Particularly noteworthy are its unusual glass roof-light with an attractive plaster roundel, and its superb wooden fittings, many of which are believed to have to come from a demolished synagogue in Leadenhall Street in the City of London.

Cheltenham had a large and thriving Hebrew community during the early 19th century, many of whom were involved in retail and the professions. Although the community is smaller nowadays, it is still significant, and this beautifully-maintained building is still regularly used for worship.

The Jewish community also maintained a small Burial Ground in Elm Street, off Tewkesbury Road, which it purchased in 1824. Although it is not usually open, some of its headstones with Hebrew inscriptions may be glimpsed through cracks in its brick walls.

TENNYSON, ALFRED LORD
Cheltenham's association with the poet extends over 6 years, covering a time when his fame had been assured but his personal happiness was threatened.

In 1837 the family left Somersby Rectory where Alfred's father had been incumbent till his death, and had moved from Lincolnshire to Epping Forest, then Tunbridge Wells and Boxley in Kent before coming to Cheltenham in 1843. They lodged first at 6 Belle Vue Place in the Upper **High Street**, taking 10 **St James' Square** after a short while. Hypochondria was afflicting the future Poet Laureate, and he went for treatment at **Prestbury**'s hydropathic establishment. In addition he was still mourning the death of his great friend, Arthur Hallam, indeed part of *In Memoriam* was written during this period, to be published in the year the Tennysons left Cheltenham, 1850.

However there were also happier events: in September 1845 the Prime Minister, Sir Robert Peel, was persuaded, after reading the poet's *Ulysses*, to recommend him a Civil List pension of £200 a year.

TERRACES

It is the mixture of individual houses with groups in terraces and crescents which gives the town both variety and cohesiveness. Fortunately there are broad streets to set off the monumental character of the terraces, so avoiding the risk of overwhelming scale. **Royal Crescent** dates from 1806 onwards, its design incorporating basement, raised groundfloor and two upper storeys, embellished with balconies and railings, setting the pattern for the rest. The only example of a convex terrace is Lansdown Crescent, built between 1831 and 1848 to a design by R.W.and C.Jearrad. Perhaps the most impressive example, though not all built at one time, is in the **Promenade**: at its centre are the **Municipal Offices**, and at the south end **Royscot House**, 1987, stands on the site formerly occupied by the **Imperial Spa** building.

Another fine example is Lansdown Terrace on the east side of Malvern Road, home of Pearson Thompson for a while, the Revd Thomas **Mozley**, a leader of the Oxford Movement, the Revd W.J.Charlton, instigator of Cheltenham's **pillar boxes**, Sir Ralph **Darling**, Governor of New South Wales, whose name is remembered by the Darling river and mountain ranges in Australia, and nearer our own time of George **Dowty**.

In St Margaret's Road, the terrace bearing the same name is unusual, if not unique, in that it was erected by the town's 'mistress builder', the Hon Katherine **Monson**.

Other examples are to be found in **Pittville, Bayshill, Montpellier** and Bath Road. Most are in the classical style with columns and cornice, but there are also instances of a reverting to Gothic details like buttresses and windows with medieval surrounds. Sometimes the chimney stacks are given special treatment, as at Lypiatt Road.

THEATRES

As would be expected in a town whose rapid expansion was due to visitors coming for the restoration of health and spirits, provision for entertainment included the theatre. However this same rapidity resulted in the early buildings' disappearance, and the total opposition of Francis **Close** to all theatres ensured that in the middle part of the 19th century there was little likelihood of replacements.

The site of Cheltenham's earliest theatre may be located in what is now Pittville Street. A converted malthouse, it saw the young Sarah Siddons performing here in 1774. By good fortune, one of David Garrick's 'talent scouts' was present and his report to the great actor resulted in Mrs Siddons leaving the humble Playhouse in Coffee House Yard and climbing the ladder as it were to fame and fortune in London. But perhaps not before she had appeared at the second Playhouse, 1782, in Grosvenor Terrace just off the **High Street**. Here **George III**'s three visits in 1788 converted it into the Theatre Royal. And here too actress Dorothy **Jordan** performed before the King.

John Boles Watson's theatre proved so successful that he opened in 1805 another larger Theatre Royal in Bath Street, and it was here that such distinguished visitors as the future George IV, the Dukes of Gloucester and Sussex, the **Duke of Wellington** and Mrs Fitzherbert enjoyed the performances. Of the actors, mention must be made of Mrs Siddons again, Charles **Macready**, Grimaldi and Edmund Kean.

But with the coming of the Revd Francis **Close** audiences declined and when a fire in 1839 destroyed the building, there was little prospect of a revival.

Perhaps the strangest surviving structure is the *Echo* Garage in St **George's Place** which still has on an inner wall the words 'Sadlers Wells'. Here a Samuel Seward gave marionette shows from 1800 to 1820, and in 1831 it was renamed the New Clarence Theatre when live shows took place.

The **Ladies' College** Princess Hall stands on the site of the Royal Well Music Hall which, as the Theatre Royal, was demolished in 1897. The **Coral's Snooker Hall** in Albion Street was once the Coliseum, but fortunately the **Playhouse** in Bath Road and the **Everyman** in Regent Street continue the town's theatrical traditions.

THIRLESTAINE HALL

Not to be confused with Thirlestaine House, which is now part of **Cheltenham College**, this extensive building stands at the junction of Thirlestaine Road and Old Bath Road. Built in the middle of the last century, the house's most conspicuous feature, a domed observatory, was not added till a Mr John Player became the owner in 1909. He had run a tin foundry in South Wales, and on moving to Cheltenham decided to follow his enthusiasm for astronomy in this practical way. When he died in 1931 the observatory presumably became derelict, indeed the whole house stood empty for some years before becoming, in 1939 an hotel, only to be occupied by the American Army Supply Service during the ensuing war.

Today it is the headquarters of the Chelsea Building Society which has aquired another intriguing oddity, the locomotive nameplate of a GWR Hall Class engine built about 40 years ago. This plaque, appropriately 'Thirlestaine Hall', needed 6 men to move it indoors to its present place in the entrance hall.

TIVOLI ROAD

Deemed by some to be one of the town's most beautiful thoroughfares by virtue of its varied architecture and range of trees, Tivoli Road also presents a rich array of history.

Many of the houses have a similarity in their fronts which can be traced to the design of J.B.**Papworth**: a central porch having on each side of it a large window crowned by a curved recess. Some villas are large, others are almost on a cottage scale. But they all display classical restraint, whether stucco or stone. However there is variety too in the presence of mews conversions, as in Cumberland Lodge and No 33a, while with No 3a there is a delightful infill between two villas, its wrought **ironwork** displaying scrolls. Perhaps the most spectacular house is St Oswalds for it is a fantasy in Gothic, its turrets and parapet, its buttresses and tracery contributing to a romantic extravagance that inevitably is a reminder of a Staffordshire ornament.

The trees too have a role in the streetscape, though not on the pavement but in the gardens: mature beeches, weeping willows, tall Scots pines, a fine Monterey cypress and most impressive of all a sequoia gigantea or Wellingtonia which rises to over 75 feet.

Then too the people who have lived in the road make interesting reading. In the last century Charles **Sturt** the explorer of Australia and General Elgee were at No 33 St Edmunds, now demolished; in the present century Ralph **Richardson** the actor was born at No 11 where later Dame Sidney Browne, first President of the College of Nursing, made her home; a neighbouring house was the residence of Princess Imeretinsky whose husband was the godson of the last Czar of Russia. On the opposite side of the road lived the composer Tony Hewitt-Jones, while further towards the Park, No 35 was the retirement home until his death in 1987 of Sir Peter Scarlett, British ambassador to Norway and the Vatican. Incidentally it was at this house in 1959 that the first instance in the country of evidence of toeprints leading to a conviction was effected. Needless to add this was when the place was a hotel and the offenders were only temporary residents!

TOWN COMMISSIONERS

Cheltenham's first real taste of local government - apart from the parish authorities - dates back to 1786, when a body of 58 Town or Paving Commissioners was appointed by Act of Parliament in order to pave, cleanse and light the streets of the developing town - a process that was, of course, underway in most English towns and cities at this time. It was under their guidance that the old market town learned to cope with the problems and potential offered by its rapid growth in the decades following 1786.

By the time of King **George III**'s visit in 1788, Cheltenham's **High**

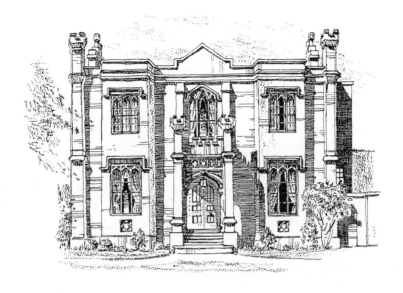

Houses in Tivoli Road

Street had been paved and lit by 120 oil lamps, and the old market buildings, which stood in the centre of the High Street, had been cleared away to help the traffic move more freely.

Ever vigilant of obstructions (everything from stray pigs to sedan chairs illegally parked on the pavement!), the Commissioners' powers were strengthened by subsequent Acts of Parliament in 1806, 1821 and 1852. They continued to serve the town until 1876, when Cheltenham received its long-awaited charter of incorporation as a Borough, and the Commissioners were replaced by a Mayor and Borough Council, which remains the basis of its system of local government today.

Eleven years later, in 1887, the town received its coat of **arms**, and chose as its motto the words *Salubritas et Eruditio*, Health and Learning, representing the two great mainstays of its prosperity in the previous 150 years, its spas and its schools.

TOWN HALL

Cheltenham's Edwardian Baroque Town Hall dominates **Imperial Square**, and is the centre of the town's cultural life, being a major venue for events during the **Festivals**, as well as of the town's regular programme of concerts and recitals. It is also the town's principal conference venue, with seating for around 1000 in its main hall.

The Town Hall was built in 1902-3, and was made necessary by the demolition, in 1900, of the **Assembly Rooms**, which had previously acted as the town's central focus. It was designed by the Gloucester architect, Frederick William Waller.

In 1906, as part of an attempt to boost Cheltenham's flagging reputation as a spa, the Corporation opened the Central Spa, to one side of the Town Hall lobby. Here, the spa waters were - and indeed still are - available to visitors, dispensed by tap from elaborate marbled urns. A taste of Cheltenham's briny waters is an essential part of any visit to the town!

The main auditorium of the Town Hall is particularly impressive and contains, in the niches on either side of the stage, large plaster cast statues of Edward VII and George V, by Boultons.

TREES

Cheltenham's finest tree-lined roads, extending from **Lansdown** to **Pittville**, are largely due to mature limes, accompanied by horse-chestnut, silver birch and plane.

For variety of species, however, a tree tour should begin in **Pittville Park**, passing on through **Wellington** and **Clarence Squares**, which have public gardens containing planes, yews and holm oaks, delightfully enclosed by hedges of mixed species.

This continues south through the town centre, where the limes and one large false acacia of **St Mary's** churchyard lead into a surviving section of Cheltenham's original **Well Walk** and to **Royal Crescent**. Since 1948 the bus station has occupied Crescent Gardens, with its two giant planes with their rookeries and two large poplars, which was Church Meadow until building began in 1805-6.

Only the **Promenade**'s upper section, alongside **Imperial Square**, still has some large horse-chestnuts, giving a 'tunnel' or esplanade effect. There is also a complete line of nine stately planes, ending with a large tulip tree in the front garden of Clarence House.

A few yards uphill lies **Montpellier Gardens** with its wellingtonia, two copper beeches, mature limes and avenue of well shaped horse-chestnuts.

Lypiatt Road, which leads south from Montpellier Rotunda, was first laid out with elms, as was Well Walk; now its frontages are defined by ivy-decked oaks, silver birch, a twin-stemmed horse-chestnut and a superb beech. Stanmer House is now a scarce example of nineteenth century landscaping: driveway, lawn and full tree screen (a yew and two fine deodar cedars). Burlington House has small yews and three holm oaks and even managed to retain its railings and gates through the wartime salvage drives.

Just south begins the thickly treed and hedged **Tivoli Road**, all achieved by private frontages, without any street trees. Here are notable beech and Scots pines, which lead through into **The Park**. A circuit of this once private drive reveals forest-sized specimens of most species and a woodland of lime and horse-chestnut screening the lake.

Grafton Road is now the town's most complete promenade of big trees (sycamores and horse-chestnuts with one beech and one plane) set in grass verges.

Returning via Park Place, the traditionally secluded grounds of The Beeches and Bicknor in **Suffolk Square** still survive. Beyond the holm oaks is the unfettered spread of Suffolk House's cedar of Lebanon, followed by limes and beeches and a pair of Lombardy poplars which used to be a characteristic urban tree in Cheltenham.

TURNPIKE ROADS

Until the early 19th century, the state of the roads around Cheltenham left much to be desired, and even as late as 1789 the road between Cheltenham and Gloucester - which had been turnpiked 30 years before - was described as 'scarcely fit for Their Majesties' servants to travel on, or pay for'.

Gradually though, the situation improved, as new Turnpike Roads were created to ease the flow of traffic to and from the town. The road to London was greatly improved, and new roads were created to Gloucester (1809), Evesham (1810) and Bath (1813), each of which soon became an important part of Cheltenham's urban topography. As with all Turnpike Roads, those using the new roads had to pay for them, and gates and toll houses were set up at the approaches to the town. These have all long since vanished, with one exception - the Beaufort Arms Inn on the London Road once served as a toll house, and part of the building has the familiar projecting bay that is characteristic of such buildings.

UNDERWOOD, GEORGE ALLEN

An architect whose short life was centred chiefly in Cheltenham and Bath, Underwood received his training from 1807 to 1815 at the London office of Sir John Soane. After initiating his own practice in Cheltenham, when he designed such buildings as **Montpellier Spa**, the **Masonic Hall, Holy Trinity Church** and the facade of the Plough Hotel, he moved to Bath on being appointed Somerset County Surveyor. He died there in 1829.

Incidentally, his brother, Charles, also became an architect, after going bankrupt as a builder, but he moved to Bristol, being responsible for some of Clifton's terraces as well as the Royal West of England Academy.

WADENOYEN, HUGO Van

The Dutch-born photographer Hugo van Wadenoyen (born 1892) lived and worked in Cheltenham from 1933 until his death in 1959, with studios in the **Promenade** (1933-56) and Rodney Road (1956-9).

Although Hugo made his living as a portrait photographer, it is for his landscapes that he is best remembered. He was one of the first photographers to reject 'pictorialism', in which photographs were made to look like engraving, in favour of direct realism in his photographs. As such, he is regarded as a pioneer of modern landscape photography, and his views of Cheltenham and the Cotswolds are amongst the finest ever taken.

WEATHER

One of the reasons for the popularity of Cheltenham amongst those retired from India was that the climate offered benefits to offset the effects of tropical living. However, weather records for the town include reports of great storms and extremes of heat and cold in the centuries of development as a fashionable spa, but it is perhaps worth looking more closely at the years in the present century when accurate instruments have been employed.

Foremost must be mentioned Cheltenham's unique position as the place where the highest temperature in the United Kingdom was registered on 3 August 1990: the town sweltered at 37.1 C or 98.8 F, exceeding that in 1911 when Cambridge achieved 36 C.

Strangely 1911 was Cheltenham's sunniest year with 2,994 hours, but 1935 was its wettest with 43' or 10.75 mm. However 1969 saw the heaviest burst of rain when on 31 May 2.5'or 62.5 mm fell in 25 minutes.

St John's Lodge, Tivoli Circus

Wellington Square

Leckhampton Court

Former turnpike at the Beaufort Arms, London Road

Floods have occurred six times since the turn of the century, 1947 being the worst, and in company with many other places Cheltenham experienced the hurricane of 1989 with winds of 90 mph, trees as might be expected suffering particularly.

The town has had its earthquakes too: one house in Bayshill Road had to be demolished as a result of a particularly noticeable tremor in 1990; and in the last century freak storms were reported - on 23 June 1843 a whirlwind over the Bath Road carried a ton of new mown hay to the top of Leckhampton Hill and as far as Andoversford, while on Sunday 16 May 1858 a short but fearsome thunderstorm struck Arle Cottage demolishing its chimney stack, shattering glass, but leaving the occupants unharmed except for one person who suffered 3" flesh removed from his shoulder and a part of his shirt embedded in the wound!

Finally a last example of Cheltenham's weather oddities: on Boxing Day 1860 a cricket match was played on the ice covering Pittville Lake.

WELL WALK

The short, but attractive pedestrian street that runs between **Clarence Street** and **St Mary's** Churchyard is a reminder of Cheltenham's earliest and most famous tree-lined avenue, the Well Walk, that was first planted with elms by Captain Henry **Skillicorne** in 1738-42.

The Well Walk began at the spa well and ran northwards to a small bridge over the **River Chelt**, where a path continued across the Church Meadow, on one side of which **Royal Crescent** was later built. The path then followed the approximate line of Crescent Place (in which stands the imposing **John Dower House**) and the street currently known as Well Walk, to reach the Churchyard and beyond that the **High Street**.

The Well Walk survived intact for a century, during which time it was trod by many thousands of visitors including royalty, aristocracy, the rich, the privileged and the famous. Eventually, however, it fell victim to the decline of the spa and the demands of developers. Parts of it were removed in the late 1830s and 1840s to make way for the new **Bayshill Estate**, while the remainder finally went in 1897, with the demolition of the **Royal Well** to make way for the Princess Hall of the **Ladies' College**.

WELLINGTON, DUKE OF

Arthur Wellesley, first Duke of Wellington, paid four visits to Cheltenham to drink the waters during the early decades of the 19th century. By all accounts, he benefited each time from his stay, and certainly Cheltenham benefited from his patronage, for it is said that he recommended the waters to many of his fellow soldiers, and thereby helped to build up Cheltenham's important links with the British army.

His first visit - as plain Arthur Wellesley - was in 1805, when he tried the waters as a cure for problems caused by a period of service in India. As well as being a purgative, the waters had a reputation for 'cooling' livers that had been disordered by the food and heat of the East, and it seems to have worked in his case, for he was back again, as a national hero, in 1816, the year after his great victory against Napoleon at Waterloo. It was during this visit that he presided at the opening of the town's new **Assembly Rooms**. Further visits were made in 1823 and 1828, the latter as Prime Minister, on which occasion he was feted in the Assembly Rooms, and welcomed to the strains of 'See, the Conquering Hero'. Cheltenham was clearly pleased to have such a prominent figure among its visitors, and the publicity value of his visit was certainly not lost on the spa's promoters!

Although 1828 was his last visit, his presence in the town is remembered by several street and house names. Cheltenham had two 'Wellington Mansions' at this time, while Wellington Street, near where he stayed, and **Wellington Square** at **Pittville** are named after him. During 1828, he is known to have visited the building works at Pittville, and it was fitting that it was a descendant, the sixth Duke, who reopened the **Pittville Pump Room** in 1960, after its period of restoration.

WELLINGTON SQUARE
Architecturally, Wellington Square is the more varied of **Pittville's** two residential Squares, and contains, on its north side, some of Pittville's earliest houses. Of these perhaps the most attractive is Glenmore Lodge, a classic small Regency villa of 1826-7, with a hint of Gothic in its windows. Facing Glenmore Lodge, and in complete contrast to it, is the red brick Eastholme of about 1870, as aggressively Victorian a house as one could ever hope to see! Also in marked contrast to Glenmore Lodge is the great Tudor-Gothic terrace on the west side of the Square, built in 1845-59; among its early residents was the actor William **Macready**, who lived at No.6 between 1860 and 1873 - it is said that Charles Dickens occasionally stayed there.

The Square's other houses conform more to the Regency 'norm' - of them, Harwood House of about 1835 is especially attractive. This, and indeed several other houses in the Square, were built by and for military families, who gravitated towards such areas as Pittville, and who helped to forge Cheltenham's close links with the British army, which it maintained well into the present century.

WILDERSPIN, SAMUEL
Although Samuel Wilderspin was born in Hornsey and died in Wakefield, his brief appearance in Cheltenham was not without significance. His life is important for its pioneering work in the development of infant schools. After starting as a clerk in a merchant's office, Wilderspin decided to

Well Walk

Statue of
Edward Wilson
in the Promenade

Wilson's boyhood
home at
The Crippets

devote himself to education. Travelling widely all over the country, he enlisted support for his cause, not least in Cheltenham where he found a convert in the Revd Francis **Close**. A Sunday school had been started in **Alstone** in 1826, and Wilderspin supervised its conversion to infant classes. Interestingly, whilst here, he lived at Alpha House in St George's Road, the same building that Dr Edward **Jenner** had used for his pioneering work in vaccination against smallpox.

WILSON, DR EDWARD ADRIAN

The Antarctic explorer, Edward Wilson, who died with Captain Scott on their return from the South Pole in March 1912, was born at 6 (now 91) Montpellier Terrace on 23 July 1872, the son of a local physician. His birthplace now has the fact of his birth there incised on its front wall.

Wilson attended **Cheltenham College**, before going to Cambridge to read Natural Science and Medicine in 1891, and although his working life was spent away from Cheltenham, he continued to regard the town as his home, returning to stay with his family whenever he could.

A talented artist, as well as a scientist, Wilson was chosen to serve as second medical officer, vertebrate zoologist and artist on Scott's 1901-4 National Antarctic Expedition (the *Discovery* expedition), on which he produced the many fine watercolours of Antarctica which are the mainstay of his artistic reputation. He subsequently served as Chief of Scientific Staff on the ill-fated 1910-13 Expedition (the *Terra Nova* expedition), and was one of the five men to reach the South Pole, in January 1912, although a combination of terrible weather, shortage of food and fuel and sickness dogged their return journey and cost all of them their lives.

Wilson is still well remembered in Cheltenham. A statue of him, sculpted by Lady Scott, was unveiled in the **Promenade** in 1914, and the **Art Gallery and Museum** has a small gallery dedicated to his life, with many of his original possessions.

WINSTON CHURCHILL MEMORIAL GARDEN

In 1829 a small orchard on the south side of Lower High Street was bought by the church authorities of **St Mary's** to be used as the New Burial Ground, because the churchyard had become overcrowded. By 1831, at a cost of £300, the chapel, still there today, had been provided in the classical style, designed by local architect, Rowland Paul. Unfortunately the original gates made by **Marshalls** have gone, though in their place there are worthy successors from the firm of **Letheren**. What have completely disappeared - though there is one in the shrubs - are the tombstones, for in 1966 the area was turned into a memorial garden. So the headstone to the much-parodied poet Nathaniel Thomas Haynes Bayley beneath a weeping willow tree provided by an admirer, Mrs Morgan, has gone, leaving him to be remembered only by a tablet in **Suffolk Square**'s **St James's Church**.

WINTER GARDENS

In 1878 Cheltenham became the proud possessor of a glass and iron Winter Gardens, complete with ornate brick towers. It was built to the design of J.T.Darby in what is now Imperial Gardens and when the **Town Hall** followed in 1901 the two places abutted each other. Whereas one succeeded the other failed. Perhaps the fashion for smaller versions of the Crystal Palace had passed. Anyway, owners came and went, each trying to promote events in its Palm Court, so in 1895 the Council took it on, putting it to such uses as auctions, circuses and roller-skating . There was even a Repertory Theatre. For a while it served as a warehouse for the **Gloster Aircraft Company**.

By 1938 the condition of the structure had deteriorated so much that it needeed only the flimsy excuse at the outbreak of war that its glass roof might attract enemy bombs for it to be demolished.

Yet strangely it has not completely gone, for the layout of the paths in the ornamental gardens indicates the position of the Winter Garden's entrances, and the tea bar still uses the base of one the towers.

WRITERS

Apart from **poets** there are associations with other writers of which Cheltenham can be proud. The enduring fantasies of Lewis Carroll owe not a little to his visit in 1863 when he stayed at the Belle Vue Hotel, taking the opportunity to see the Liddell family at **Charlton Kings** - a family which included of course Alice. Also at Charlton Kings mention must be made of Mrs Craik who wrote part of her *John Halifax, Gentleman* there. Anthony Trollope lived in Paragon Terrace, Bath Road for a short time during his career as a Post Office surveyor; Charles Dickens and Jane Austen came here; Fanny Burney as lady-in-waiting to Queen Charlotte would have spent those momentous weeks in Cheltenham's history when **George III** took the 'water cure' here. In 1830 young John Ruskin lodged in the **High Street** with his parents, though his great works on architecture and painting had yet to be written.

Other writers still in their formative years came to **Cheltenham Ladies' College,** among them being D.K.Broster, Margaret Kennedy and Mary Sinclair. Some writers already established here used the town as settings for their work: Thackeray's *Vanity Fair* and Bulwer Lytton's *Pelham* have been followed by others in contemporary works which have incorporated such places as the racecourse and **GCHQ**.

And inevitably the **Festivals** of Literature have attracted so many luminaries of the writers' firmament that their listing would almost amount to an index of literary history.